CRITICAL THINKING BIBLE

PROBLEM-SOLVING SKILLS | EFFECTIVE
DECISION-MAKING | IMPROVE YOUR REASONING |
OVERCOME NEGATIVE THOUGHTS |
INDEPENDENT THINKING

MICHAEL GATES

FOREWORD

We are in a day and age where self-development is a must at a certain point in our lives, whether it is to better ourselves on a professional or personal level. Therefore, many people undergo this journey to return from it as a much more developed person who can deal with and understand problems, think for themselves, be more productive, and spend their time learning new things to stimulate their brains, triggering various hormone releases that bring joy or satisfaction. With this in mind, it is safe to say that this journey certainly is not an easy one, as it takes a lot of time for a person to change, as no one has ever changed over twenty-four hours.

Critical thinking is one of the bigger things a person should learn in their life, as it revolves around many important topics, and it connects to many other topics, forming a chain of knowledge and various skills that can aid you in becoming a better person. For example, it can provide you with a plethora of ways to deal with problems in calm and adequate ways without panicking, help you find ways to stimulate your mind and boost your memory and learning abilities, increase your self-discipline and productivity so you can get more done in a shorter amount of time, how to efficiently make decisions, especially in a professional environment where said skill is very valued by many professionals, become better at reasoning. It can also help you become a more independent thinker, which is a very valuable asset in this age. Still, it can also help you learn how to generate, store and synthesize knowledge properly.

With the introduction out of the way, it is time to take a leap and begin this journey of self-development, to learn about critical thinking and the many branches and various topics that tie into it, making it a valuable asset that you can use to achieve more in life and become a better version of yourself.

ONE

DEFINING CRITICAL THINKING – WHAT IT IS AND WHY YOU NEED IT

Critical thinking can be seen as a very rich and diverse concept that has been in development for roughly the past 2,500 years. The roots of the term stem from the mid to late twentieth century, and with time, it is safe to say that there are many definitions of the term, most of them even overlapping and making it more difficult to grasp the concept via definition.

1.1 What is critical thinking?

One way critical thinking can be defined is "an intellectually disciplined process which includes active and skillful conceptualization, application, analysis, synthesis and/or evaluation of gathered information generated by, or gathered from, observing, reflecting, experiencing, reasoning and communicating, seen as a guide to action and belief." Thus, the base of critical thinking revolves around intellectual values that go beyond those among the lines of subject matter divisions, such as precision, clarity, accuracy, relevance, consistency, concrete evidence, depth, breadth, solid reasoning, and fairness.

Critical thinking entails the examining of the afore-mentioned structures, or elements, of thought which is implicit in all reasoning: problems, purposes, or question-at-issue, concepts, assumptions, empirical grounding, implications and consequences, reasoning which leads to conclusions, frame of reference, and objections from differing viewpoints. Despite being responsive to subject matters, purposes, and issues that may vary, critical thinking is incorporated into a family of intercalated modes of thinking, such as scientific thinking, mathematical thinking, anthropological thinking, economic thinking, moral thinking, and historical and philosophical thinking.

We can safely say that critical thinking can be split up into two main components: 1) a set of information, processing skills, and belief generating skills, and 2) using the aforementioned skills, based solely on intellectual commitment and the habit of doing so. Henceforth, they are contrasted with: 1) the simple obtaining and retaining of information itself, as it revolves around a particular way in which information is treated and sought; 2) simply possessing a set of skills, as it involves their continual use, and 3) the usage of said skills with a lack of acceptance to the produced results.

It is also worth mentioning that critical thinking can change depending on the motivation behind it. When the motivation behind it lies beneath ulterior, selfish motives, it can be commonly manifested in the forms of skillful idea manipulation, resulting in benefits or services for the general interest of a single person or a group of people. Thus, critical thinking is said to be very flawed on an intellectual note, despite how realistic and successful it may be. However, when the motive behind critical thinking lies beneath intellectual integrity and fairness of mind, it can be considered an intellectuality of a higher order, even though it is often subjected to being called "idealism" by those who use it for selfish purposes.

It is important to know that, despite critical thinking being a universal word and having a generalized definition, it is not the same within every individual. Every human being is always subject to moments of irrational or mal-disciplined thought. Therefore, the quality of critical thinking heavily revolves around a degree, quality, and depth of experience in a certain domain of thinking, or concerning types of questions, among many other things. Thus, it is safe to say that no human being can be, or is, a critical thinker through and through, all through and through, and such-and-such insights, and is subject to certain is-and-such tendencies towards some form of self-deception. Henceforth, we can say that the development of critical thinking is a process that can take up to a lifetime.

The importance and value of critical thinking can be derived by considering these points: every human being and animal thinks, as it is but second nature to us. However, it is valuable knowledge that the thinking of every human being can be very subjective, skewed, it can encompass a small fragment, or it can revolve solely around prejudice. With this in mind, it is safe to say that the quality of life we lead and what we make and produce relies on the quality of our thoughts. Negligent and poor thinking can lead to cuts, both financially and in quality of life. On another note, excellent and careful thought leads to positive benefits, but it must be adequately and properly nurtured. This defines the problem that critical thinking most commonly solves within people: poor thought processes and decisions.

. . .

A way to circumvent the problems caused by the lack of critical thinking is by doing our best to become diligent and excellent critical thinkers. Those can pose very vital questions and properly and formulate and articulate them. Critical thinkers of adequate nature can also properly and efficiently gather even abstract ideas and information and interpret them before coming to conclusions by testing them with comparison to standards and relevant criteria. Developed critical thinkers can be open-minded within different systems of thought, possessing the capability to assess and recognize, based on their needs, their implications, practical consequences, and assumptions. Finally, a great critical thinker is experienced in effective communication with other individuals or groups, especially in attempting to obtain solutions to problems of varying complexities.

In simpler terms, critical thinking can be defined as the self-monitored, self-directed, self-disciplined, and self-corrective thinking of an individual. It often implies approval to very high standards of excellence and their mindful command and usage. It also entails effective problem solving and communication abilities and a commitment to overcoming the notions of sociocentrism and egocentrism.

1.2 The intellectual roots of critical thinking

The source of critical thinking is as old as its etymology, and it can be traced back to the teaching practice of 2500 years ago and Socrates' vision. Through questioning and inquiry, he found that people could not reasonably prove their assertion of knowledge. Confusing meanings, conflicting beliefs, or insufficient evidence are often hidden under mild but mostly empty rhetoric. Socrates established that one could not rely on those with "authority" to obtain sound knowledge and insight. It shows that people can have power and high positions, but they can also be confused and irrational. He established the importance of asking insightful questions that explore ideas before they can be considered credible. He established the importance of finding evidence, carefully examining reasoning and hypotheses, analyzing basic concepts, and tracking what is said and the meaning of what is done. His questioning method is now called "Socratic questioning" and is the most famous critical thinking teaching strategy. In his question, Socrates emphasized the need to think clearly and logically.

Socrates set the agenda for the critical thinking tradition, that is, to reflexively question common beliefs and interpretations, and carefully distinguish between those that are reasonable and logical, and those, no matter how attractive they are to our original egocentrism Power, no matter how attractive they are. Serve our self-centeredness. No matter how comfortable or comforting the vested interests are, they lack sufficient evidence or rational basis to prove our beliefs.

Socrates' "practice" is followed by the critical thinking of Plato (which records Socrates' thoughts), Aristotle, and Greek skeptics. They all emphasize that things are often very different from what they seem. In the same way, only trained minds are prepared to see through the way things see us on the surface (deceptive appearances) to the way they are hidden below the surface (the deeper reality of life). From this ancient Greek tradition, anyone who desires to understand a deeper level of reality, systematic thinking, and tracing its meaning extensively and deeply needs it because only comprehensive, well-founded, and well-founded ideas that can respond to objections can take us beyond the surface.

In the Middle Ages, systematic critical thinking was reflected in the writings and teachings of thinkers such as Thomas Aquinas (Summa Theologica). To ensure his thinking passed the critical thinking test, he always systematically stated, thought, and responded to everyone criticizing their ideas, thinking that this is a necessary stage for their development. St. Thomas

Aquinas raised our awareness of the potential power of reasoning and raised our awareness of the need to cultivate and "re-examine" reasoning systematically. Of course, Aquino's thinking also shows that people who think critically do not always reject established beliefs but only those that lack reasonable grounds.

During the Renaissance (15th and 16th centuries), many European scholars began to think critically about religion, art, society, human nature, law, and freedom. They continue to assume that most areas of human life require careful analysis and criticism. Among these scholars are the British Colet, Erasmus, and Moore. They followed the perception of the ancients.

Francis Bacon from the UK was concerned about the way we abuse our minds to pursue knowledge. He realized that the mind could not safely leave its natural inclination. In his book "Progress in learning," he demonstrated the importance of studying the world empirically. He emphasized the information-gathering process and laid the foundation for modern science. He also drew attention to the fact that most people, if allowed to develop, will develop bad habits of thought (which he calls "idols"), leading them to believe in false or misleading things. He drew attention to "tribal idols" (the way our minds naturally tend to deceive ourselves), "market idols" (the way we abuse words), "theater idols" (we tend to fall into the traditional ideological system), and the "school idols" (Based on blind rules and poorly oriented thinking problems). His book can be considered one of the first texts on critical thinking because his agenda is largely the traditional agenda of critical thinking.

In France, some 50 years later, Descartes wrote what might be called a second text on critical thinking, "The rules of the direction of the mind." In it, Descartes defended the need for special and systematic mental training to guide its thoughts. He clarified and defended the need for clear and accurate thinking. He developed a critical thinking method based on the principle of systematic skepticism. He emphasized the need to base ideas on a well-thought-out foundation through basic assumptions. He believes that every part of thinking should be questioned, doubted, and tested. During the same period, Sir Thomas Moore developed a model of a new social order, a utopia, in which every area of the world today is criticized. His implicit argument is that the established social system requires radical analysis and criticism. The critical thinking of these Renaissance and post-Renaissance scholars paved the way for the emergence of science and the development of democracy, human rights, and freedom of thought.

During the Italian Renaissance, Prince Machiavelli criticized the politics of the time and laid the foundation for modern critical political thought. He refuses to assume that the government operates as claimed by those in power. On the contrary, he critically analyzed how it worked and laid the foundations of political thought, exposing the true agenda of politicians on the one hand and on the other hand exposing many contradictions and inconsistencies in the cruel and cruel world. The Politics of His Time

In England in the 16th and 17th centuries, Hobbes and Locke showed the same confidence in the critical thinking of thinkers that we find in Machiavelli. Nor does he accept the traditional ideas that dominated thought at the time. Both believe that what is considered "normal" in their culture is necessarily rational. They both hope that critical thinking opens up new learning perspectives. Hobbes adopted a naturalistic worldview in which everything can be explained by evidence and reasoning. Locke advocated a common-sense analysis of daily life and thought. He laid a theoretical foundation for critically thinking about basic human rights and the responsibility of all governments to accept reasonable criticism from thoughtful citizens.

In this spirit of intellectual freedom and critical thinking, people like Robert Boyle (17th century) and Sir Isaac Newton (17th and 18th century) accomplished their work. Among his skeptical chemists, Boyle severely criticized his previous chemical theories. In turn, Newton developed a powerful ideological framework that comprehensively criticized the traditionally accepted worldview. Moreover, he expanded the critical thinking of Copernicus, Galileo, and Kepler. After Boyle and Newton, those who seriously reflect on the natural world realized that they must abandon the self-centered worldview and instead support a view based solely on carefully collected evidence and reasonable reasoning.

Another important contribution of critical thought was the French Enlightenment thinkers: Baylor, Montesquieu, Voltaire, and Diderot. They all start from the premise that the human mind can better understand the nature of the social and political world when limited by reason. More importantly, reason must turn to itself to determine the strengths and weaknesses of thinking for these thinkers. They value disciplined knowledge exchanges, and all opinions must be carefully analyzed and criticized. They believe that all authorities must be examined in one way or another through reasonable critical challenges.

18th-century thinkers have further expanded our understanding of critical thinking and cultivated our understanding of the power of critical thinking and its tools. Applied to economic issues, it produced Adam Smith's "The Wealth of Nations." In the same year, using the traditional concept of allegiance to the king, the "Declaration of Independence" was published. It then produced Kant's Critique when applied to reason itself.

In the nineteenth century, Comte and Spencer further extended critical thinking to the realm of human social life. Applied to the problem of capitalism, it produced a profound social and economic critique of Karl Marx. Applied to the history of human culture and biological life, it led to Darwin's human origin. Applied to the subconscious, it is reflected in the works of Sigmund Freud. Applied to culture, it led to the establishment of the field of anthropological research. Applied to language, it led to many in-depth discussions in linguistics and the functions of signs and language in human life.

In the 20th century, our understanding of the power and nature of critical thinking had emerged in ever clearer expressions. In 1906, William Graham Sumner (William Graham Sumner) published a pioneering study on the foundations of sociology and anthropology, "Folklore," which recorded the trend of human thought in centered social thought and parallel trends in the (noncritical) functional services that schools instill in society:

"Schools make everyone follow a model, that is, orthodoxy. Unless regulated by the best knowledge and good conscience, school education will produce men and women who all belong to a pattern, just like a lathe. All great doctrines about life have an orthodoxy. It consists of the oldest and most common opinions commonly seen among the masses. Popular opinions always contain wide-ranging fallacies, half-truths, and simple generaliza-tions (p. 630).

At the same time, Sumner recognizes the deep need for critical thinking in life and education:

"Criticism is the inspection and testing of any accepted propositions to find out whether they are in line with reality. Critical teachers are the product of educa-tion and training. It is a habit of thinking, but also a kind of power. The training of men and women in this area is the first condition for human well-being. This is our only guarantee against deception, deceit, superstition, and misunderstanding of ourselves and our earthly environ-ment. Education is good because it can cultivate critical teachers who start. Teachers of any subject, if they insist on precision and reasonable control of all processes and methods and are open to unlimited verification and modification, this method cultivates students' habits. Educated people cannot be stamped. They could not believe it for a long time. They can keep things as possible or possible in every way, without certainty and pain. They can wait for evidence and weigh it. They can resist appeals to their dearest prejudices. Critical teacher education is the only education that can truly be a good citizen".

John Dewey agreed. From his work, we have strengthened the practical foundation of human thought (its instrumentality) Awareness, especially its foundation in humanity's real purpose and goals. Building on the work of Ludwig Wittgenstein, we have not only increased our awareness of the importance of concepts in human thought, but we have also increased the need to analyze concepts and assess their strengths and limitations. Building on Piaget's work, we have improved our understanding of the egocentric and social-centered tendency of human thought and the special needs for developing critical thinking, which can reason from multiple angles and improve to the level of "conscious realization." From the great contributions of all the hard sciences, we understand the power of information and the importance of collecting information with care and precision. We remain sensitive to its possible inaccuracies, distortions, or misuse. From the contribution of psychology In-depth, we learned how easy it is for human thought to delude itself, how easy it is to build hallucinations and delusions in the unconscious, how easy it is to rationalize and stereotype, plan and scapegoat.

In short, the history of thought Critical thinkers has become a tool and a scapegoat. Resources have increased enormously. Several hundreds of great minds and thinkers have contributed to its development. Every major discipline has made some contributions to critical thinking. However, for most educational purposes, the most important thing is summarizing the basic common denominator of critical thinking.

1.3 Why do independent thinkers do it better? – the benefits

An intellectually active mind opens the door of opportunity. Whether your thinking is on the wavelength of logic or creativity, you can improve performance, productivity, efficiency, and achieve a higher level of self-awareness as an independent thinker. Independent thinking is a tool that can be used to enhance personal expression and creativity and is a valuable additional skill.

Many factors promote independent thinking. However, high self-esteem is the most distinguishing characteristic of any creative thinker and is usually the driving force for personal thinking, performance, and success. Everyone's feelings about themselves can be both restrictive and inspiring, so they must show a good level of self-awareness. Without self-acceptance, personal progress will be greatly slowed down. Therefore, to encourage positive self-expression, awareness must be raised.

Self-confidence can also be generated externally through the thoughts and comments of others. Although this is effective for increasing ability and confidence, it should not replace personal self-esteem built by believing in one's abilities. Therefore, all successful independent thinkers have a clear understanding of self-worth.

Some of the qualities of independent thinkers are persistence, belief, independent self-esteem, self-confidence, determination, and creative consciousness. These and other qualities will make your thinking more innovative and help you create the best opportunity to demonstrate independent thinking positively.

Committing to developing these qualities will also inspire individuals to explore their ways of thinking and remove the limitations and limitations that their current thinking patterns have established. As your personal qualities develop, independent thinking will begin to flow more freely.

Being able to think independently opens up a wealth of potential insights. For example, it makes you more sensitive to what you hear, see, and believe and helps you question values and assumptions. Independent thinking can also hone your skills on many other levels, including building confidence in your ability to stand up for your beliefs.

1.4 Are there barriers to critical thinking? – the challenges

As with any sphere of personal development, there are several types of obstacles to critical thinking that hamper a person's personality and their personality in general. Due to these factors, people cannot operate efficiently in a business environment. In this chapter, we will discuss some of the more common factors that can be seen as challenges faced during critical thinking.

Self-centered nature or behavior is a natural tendency that is difficult to overcome in many cases. This barrier makes people think about themselves and makes it impossible to empathize with others to understand their problems and problems. You can be one of the biggest obstacles to critical thinking yourself. It is seen as more of a personality defect; despite various attempts to change, it is difficult for a person to change. These people can not evaluate the opinions and feelings of others and make others feel uncomfortable working with them as a team.

. . .

Group thinking is still one of the most harmful obstacles to critical thinking, and it is also very unhealthy. In this case, this person has no opinion or decision of his own in any situation or situation. To overcome the same problems, everyone on the team needs to stand up, questioning and expounding their ideas, opinions, and ideas.

The so-called "drone mindset" (also known as "drone mentality") can be explained as a person's inattention in important work meetings and discussions. It will affect anyone who influences the critical thinking process at any time. In many cases, ordinary daily life will make a person a victim of the drone mindset. For example, company managers and human resources departments must keep employees interested in challenging tasks and motivations.

Many of us have the habit of thinking in our comfort zone. We even avoid thinking outside of our range because we are taught to think in a certain way due to various social conditions. Critical thinking obstacles caused by social conditions include stereotypes about the things and people around us and unnecessary assumptions that make it difficult for people around us to work in the organization. Overcoming such behaviors and obstacles requires cultural and social awareness.

Personal bias is one of the biggest obstacles to critical thinking because it slows down and prevents a person from making fair, open, and transparent decisions. It also prevents people from using logical reasoning, experience, and basic common sense to make wise and effective decisions.

Often in our workplace, we are tired of strict deadlines, which affect our critical thinking skills. But the positive side is that a person can also improve their critical thinking skills and abilities within a difficult and tight time frame. When time is short and needs to be completed before the deadline, we often choose to complete the job without any strategic thinking or long-term vision. This is when the barriers to critical thinking arise.

Arrogance is a bad attitude that, more often than not, hampers critical thinking skills. It makes a person have a closed mind and think that they know everything and no longer need to learn new things. As a result, arrogance can cause a person to fail for a long time because it closes the learning channel and cannot assess the rewards and benefits of critical thinking.

One of the obstacles to critical thinking is stubborn nature because people with this nature have their own beliefs and ideologies. This barrier is not popular in the business world, especially in the business world, because it is constantly evolving and dynamic in nature and methodology. This person must be open to change and leave behind their current beliefs, understanding that the business world is fluid and fast-paced, requiring flexibility and adaptability.

Fear is often an obstacle to critical thinking and an obstacle to a person's overall growth and development. The fear made him feel insecure, lost motivation, and unable to think outside the box flexibly and come up with ideas and strategies. Fear can be caused by various reasons, such as anxiety, depression, self-esteem issues, and other personal reasons that affect a person's career.

Critical thinking requires a person to do a lot of research, study work-related literature, and be willing to learn new things to promote growth and development. But when a person is lazy, it becomes one of the obstacles to critical thinking.

With all of this said, it is important to know that there are, in fact, many more factors which affect critical thinking - the ones mentioned above are only the most common ones that you may face, meaning that you should still do a certain amount of research to find out more about the potential barriers in critical thinking.

1.5 Where to start your personal development

Whether in a personal or professional context, the importance and necessity of good decision-making cannot be denied. As mentioned before, critical thinking can help us find flaws (if any) in a decision-making process and helps us achieve better results by eliminating these flaws. In short, no matter what you are doing, you must have that set of decision-making skills; For this, you must be able to think critically and act quickly. Listed below will be several steps you can take to get one step closer to becoming a better and more seasoned critical thinker.

Know exactly what you want. Knowing what your needs are is the first step in critical thinking. We must think critically and solve problems so that we may reach our goals. Every decision we make has an additional goal or purpose, and we determine exactly what it is and what we want from it, providing us with a starting point for work. So ask yourself: "What do I want?" or "What do I hope to get out of this endeavor?" unless you know the answers to these questions, you will not know which is the correct decision.

Come face-to-face with your biases. Often, we only think and deal with problems from our perspectives. However, if you try to think from someone else's perspective, it helps with critical thinking and decision-making. In addition, it allows you to understand the general situation more clearly. Suppose you want to solve a problem at work. Think about how your best friend will approach you or how your partner or siblings will be. Now think about how your boss will handle it. Allow yourself to consider different points of view, and you may find solutions you have not considered before.

Consider all the consequences of each available option. Every choice we make will affect us or may affect others involved in the problem. Therefore, you must weigh the possible consequences of each of your choices and choose the most beneficial one while limiting the negative impact on others. A good way is to write a list of pros and cons. By allowing yourself to consider all possible positive outcomes and possible negative outcomes, you can make more informed decisions.

Do adequate and extensive research. You have most likely heard thousands of times by now that "knowledge is power." However, many of us tend to rely heavily on what we already know and are unwilling to give up our own beliefs. Critical thinking sometimes requires you to give up your beliefs to solve problems. Unwillingness to learn, research, or gain new beliefs will only stop you and certainly will not help you to think critically. By spending time investigating and focusing on learning, you will find that over time you will evolve and adapt to overcome new situations and improve your critical thinking.

Learn to accept that you may not always be right. This may come as a pill that is very difficult to swallow. It is okay to make mistakes; no matter who we are, we all make them. However, most of us do not accept this fact that prevents us from thinking critically. If you do something wrong and keep doing it repeatedly because you have assumed it will never go wrong, then this needs to be changed for your benefit. Always check for potential solutions to problems, consider new options, and treat mistakes as opportunities for learning.

Breaking things down and simplifying them. It is great to see the big picture, but if you can break things down into smaller parts, so much the better. The reason is that the smaller the part is, the easier it is to digest and absorb and then use mentally. Dealing with many little things is much easier than trying to solve a big picture that can become unwieldy. Try to think in terms of steps: "What should I do first?" - make a list and try to organize them in order of priority or time. By dividing a big problem into several parts, you can start looking for a solution instead of spending half your time on this problem.

Stop overcomplicating things. Overcomplicating things is something that many of us have in common. Yes, it may be necessary to think carefully about things, but you will only make things more difficult if you start thinking too much. You have to discover the subtle difference between positive thinking and overthinking. There are several situations where the job can be done simply.

·   ·   ·

It is important to know that if you still have questions about your critical thinking skills - you are not alone, as critical thinking is by no means an easy task. Sometimes it will require you to give up what you believe in and come up with new ideas. It can be challenging at times, but it is all worth it if you do it right!

TWO
BUILDING YOUR CRITICAL THINKER TOOLKIT

As with every attempt at becoming a better human being, one must understand that a certain set of skills is needed, both in a mental, physical, and even professional field. To be a good mathematician, you have to have studied thousands of examples and equations but still gotten stuck on some of them for several days. To be a good chemist, you must have done several hundred, if not thousands, of experiments in a laboratory, failing some on the way. To be a good literature teacher, you must have spent thousands of hours reading, analyzing, and taking notes of various paragraphs for future reference but still failed in deciphering that one sentence in a five hundred page book.

Simply put, to develop critical thinking, much like any other discipline, you must first know what skill set or tools you will need to achieve this goal.

2.1 The main skills of a critical thinker

As with every other life skill, there is no universal standard for the skills included in the critical thinking process. With that in mind, we have narrowed it down to the following six items. Focusing on them can put you on the path to becoming an outstanding critical thinker.

The first step in the critical thinking process is identifying the situation or problem and the factors that might affect it. Once you have a clear understanding of the situation and the people, groups, or factors that may be affected, you can begin to delve into the problem and its possible solutions. When faced with a new situation, problem or scenario, stop and take a mental inventory of the situation and ask the following questions: "Who is doing what?", "What is the reason for this situation?" "What is the end result, and how will they change?" and proceed to deduce from there.

The ability to do independent research is key when comparing arguments on a topic. Arguments are meant to be persuasive, meaning that the facts and data in your favor may lack context or come from questionable and non-reliable sources. The best way to solve this problem is independent verification, finding the source of information, and evaluating it. One way to circumvent this is by cultivating attention to no-source claims - did the person presenting the argument provide information about where they got this information? If you ask or try to find it yourself, and there is no clear answer, you should treat it as a red flag. It is also important to know that not all sources are equally valid; take the time to understand the difference between popular and scholarly articles.

Recognizing biases can be very difficult because even the smartest of us may not recognize bias. However, strong critical thinkers will do their best to evaluate information objectively. Think of yourself as a judge because you want to evaluate the arguments of both parties in the dispute, but you also need to remember the biases that each party may have. Setting aside your personal bias is equally important, but it may be a much more difficult process than you think. Potrafka once said, "You must have the courage to debate and argue with your ideas and assumptions," and "'This is essential for learning to look at things from a different perspective." Try to challenge yourself consistently, find the evidence that constitutes your beliefs, and assess whether your source of information is credible.

First, you should be aware of the potential existence

of biases. When evaluating information or arguments in relation to biases, ask yourself the following questions: "Who benefits from it?", "Does the source of this information have any hidden purpose?", "Does the source ignore or omit information that does not support its beliefs or claims?" and "Does this source use unnecessary language to influence the viewer's view of the facts?".

The ability to reason and draw conclusions based on the information provided, known as reasoning, is another important skill for mastering critical thinking. The information is not always accompanied by a summary explaining its meaning, meaning that you should evaluate the information provided and draw conclusions based on the original data. Inference capabilities allow you to infer and discover potential outcomes when evaluating scenarios. It is also important to note that not all inferences are correct. For example, if you read that someone weighs 105 pounds, you could infer that they are underweight or unhealthy. However, other data points such as height and body composition may change this conclusion.

Reasoning is an educated guess. You can hone your ability to reason correctly by consciously gathering as much information as possible and then drawing conclusions. When faced with a new scene or situation to evaluate, first try to find clues (such as headlines, featured images, and statistics), and then be sure to ask yourself what you think is happening.

One of the most challenging parts of critical thinking in challenging scenarios is figuring out what information is most important to you. In many cases, you will see information that seems important, but in the end, it may be just a secondary piece of information that needs to be considered.

The best way to better determine relevance is to establish a clear direction on what you are trying to figure out. Is your task to find a solution? Should you identify a trend? If you have determined the end goal, you can use it to determine what is relevant. However, even with clear goals, it is difficult to determine which information is truly relevant. One strategy to solve this problem is to make a physical list of data points in order of relevance. When you view it this way, you may get a list that contains a few related pieces of information at the top of the list and some information at the bottom that you may be able to ignore. From there, you can narrow your focus to less clear topics in the middle of the list for further evaluation.

· · ·

It is very easy to sit back and accept the superficial value of everything presented to you, but when faced with a scene that requires critical thinking, it can also lead to disaster. In fact, we are curious beings by nature - just ask any parent who is faced with the "Why?" from their children. With age, it is easier to develop the habit of suppressing the need to ask questions. But this is not a successful method of critical thinking.

Although curiosity seems innate to you, you can still train yourself to cultivate this curiosity effectively. Just consciously ask open-ended questions about things you see in your daily life, and then you can take the time to follow up on these questions.

Critical thinking is essential for anyone who wants to have a successful college career and a productive professional life after graduation. Your ability to objectively analyze and evaluate complex issues and situations will always be helpful. Unleash your potential by practicing and honing the six critical thinking skills listed above. Most professionals attribute their time in college to the key to developing critical thinking skills. If you want to improve your skills in a way that can affect your future life and career, then higher education is a great place.

2.2 It is all in the mind: what is the correct mentality to achieve your goals

When you decide to accept a profound life change, it is scary because change is scary. But the only way to successfully cope with change is to master it. Once you get the hang of it, your life will move on easily and naturally.

One of the first things you can start by doing is to take the time to define your vision and passion. If you do not see something now, who knows whether you will be able to see it again in the future ever again. So take a few steps out of your comfort zone. Experiment, feel, and taste what you are passionate about. Get out there and find yourself, what you stand for and what you oppose. Then ask yourself what you want and why it is important to you. Find out what excites you. Your vision should focus on you and your desires only. It must be complete, clear, and cruel honesty.

People are often lazy; they have only a pale vision of what they want. Try to stop and take a break from your daily running. Take a notebook, choose a quiet time and place, write down what you particularly want to accomplish and how you know when it is done. Write everything down—your brain will do whatever you want, but you must be very clear about your mission to do this. So start writing down your dreams in detail to better visualize the process and steps needed to achieve those dreams.

You usually know what you want, but you may start to lose motivation after writing for a while. That is when you slow down and fall into depression. Sometimes, you need to reach outside of your bounds to make the most of your slump. Ask yourself: "Who is affected by my dreams?" or "Who can benefit from it?". Think of all your relatives. How will they be affected one year after their dream is realized? What about two years? You are getting stronger and stronger, the interests of your loved ones are getting bigger and bigger, and the influence on the communities around you is expanding. Imagine how all of this will add up in five years, or even ten. Maintain focus on the vision in your head and feel the energy. Whenever you notice yourself losing motivation, always retrace your thoughts and remember where you started, why you are on this journey of self-development, and how those around you will benefit or be affected by these changes.

How will you realize your dream? What are the complete skills you need? What new knowledge is needed to proceed? One of the easiest ways to create a roadmap for your dream trip is to model the behavior of people who have successfully achieved what you want to achieve. Find those people. Interview them if possible. Read your trip. Copy their steps. Learn from their experiences. This will make your plans have more shape and definition, making it substantially easier for you to take your first steps on your journey.

Our beliefs are external (or what we say aloud) and internal (or feelings deep inside us). Inner beliefs usually determine how you truly feel about yourself, who you are, and what your abilities consist of. Saying you will run a marathon when you think you will not even be able to breathe after five miles is not a victory. The good news is that beliefs can be rewritten through diligent inner work: meditation, daily affirmation, journaling, creative imagination. Use whatever works for you. Remember, belief drives perception, perception drives habit, and habit drives action and success. You are what you think.

To be proficient in one thing, you must have perseverance and discipline. This includes brainpower, establishing and following a set of daily habits needed to achieve goals, and 2) paying great attention to distractions.

Your current habits are specifically designed to help you accomplish all the things you have done. If you want something new, you must make drastic changes to your current habits. So in the process of pursuing your dreams, what new habits can you establish for yourself?

Discipline also means developing distraction alerts. Not only do you have to keep your habits, but you also have to make a conscious decision to achieve the right thing and stay away from the ineffective. Multitasking is just a modern myth. The fact is that the most successful people are focused.

By constantly performing seemingly small actions, you sow the seeds of achievement in your consciousness. You begin to feel the progress you are making, and over time these feelings will become a belief and then an attitude.

2.3 Where to look for mental stimulation

Mental activity or nerve stimulation can be described as anything that stimulates, activates, or enriches the mind. The stimulus can be provided from within the mind or from outside the environment. Education, career, social, and leisure activities are important factors for mental stimulation. As healthy as it is for the body on a physical level, mental activity or mental stimulation is a great way of making sure that you are staying active on a higher cognitive level, but also satisfying your mental cravings instead of spending time aimlessly watching videos or playing games on your computer or console. Below you will be able to find some interesting ways of stimulating your mind to boost your capabilities.

Try using your non-dominant hand. If you are right-handed, you become left-handed that day. Changing the simple behavior of your hands that you normally use for daily tasks will make your brain think differently. When brushing your teeth, use your other hand. Eating? Use the opposite hand. You can challenge yourself and try to use your least used handwriting throughout the day.

Start talking to yourself. Pick a time a day to discuss anything verbally with yourself. Use your voice to describe what you see, what you are doing, your plans for the evening or dinner you want to make, rather than keeping it in your mind. Of course, you can sound like a lunatic, which makes this activity better when you are alone, but talking while you think is a great boost to the brain. In addition, you can find a solution to a problem that you have been trying to solve; Sometimes, expressing stress can make you sleep better at night.

3. Write down your dreams. You can write down wishes and goals as reminders, but having a pencil and paper by your bedside to record your dreams is a fun way to get your brain thinking. In addition to improving memory, uncovering the mystery and hidden meaning behind the sleepy brain is also a way to understand yourself and your brainpower better.

Deprive yourself of your visual senses when taking a shower or bath. Your senses help your brain make decisions and make connections, but we often rely too heavily on one or two senses and leave others behind. Stimulate your brain and close your eyes when you wash your hair, eat, or put on clothes. In addition to being a fun challenge, your brain is encouraged to use other senses that have been forgotten.

Start incorporating physical activity in your daily life. Like the body, our brain also needs physical exercise. Walking steadily will increase blood circulation, which will promote the growth of blood vessels in the brain and improve energy production and waste elimination. Plus, it is easy to walk, and you can do it anytime, anywhere.

Park your car further away from work or take time to walk around the block at the end of the day. As you clear your mind, you will get into nature, which is good for your brain.

THREE
MASTERING SELF-DISCIPLINE

Self-discipline is necessary to achieve optimal health by breaking habits (for example, smoking) or rebalancing the health problems caused by excessive eating. Self-discipline gives you the drive and motivation to focus on your goals. It allows you to maintain control over yourself and your reaction to any situation. Simply put, it is like a muscle: the more you train, the stronger you will become. Conversely, lack of self-discipline can lead to low self-esteem.

Many research articles state that self-discipline is capable of predicting academic success better than IQ. One study found that highly self-disciplined teens outperformed their more impulsive peers on all academic performance variables, including transcript grades, standardized achievement test scores, highly competitive high school admission, and attendance.

Self-discipline encompasses making wise decisions. The food you eat to the amount of exercise you do depends on your discipline. For example, exercise can promote a sense of control over the body, which can translate into a better sense of control over other aspects of life, which is the key to resisting stress. People who exercise regularly show higher levels of self-esteem and maintain self-discipline. The five pillars of self-discipline are acceptance, willpower, hard work, diligence, and perseverance.

Acceptance is the most basic challenge people face. They cannot accurately perceive and accept their current situation. It is important to identify the weakest areas of your subject. Assess where you are now. Acknowledge and accept your starting point, and design a plan for yourself to improve in this area. Willpower is a concentration of power. Choose your goal. Develop an attack plan and execute it. When you are feeling stressed, your willpower is at its lowest. Hard work is something many people try to avoid by doing the simplest things. But strong challenges are often related to strong results. Diligence is developing the ability to invest time and energy. With proper development of diligence, you will insist that you can continue to act even if you have no motivation to keep accumulating results. Persistence will follow soon after, and it will provide its own motivation. When combined with goal setting, passion, and planning, self-discipline can become very powerful. Write down your goals again, and make sure you do your best to meet them. Before moving on to another task, be sure to complete the tasks that you set. For some people, the idea of setting goals can feel overwhelming. Seek support so that you too can experience the satisfaction of achieving goals that are important to you.

3.1 How to control your emotions and impulses

There is an insurmountable difference between doing things that make you feel good at the moment and doing things that make you feel good after said moment has passed. It may feel good to be under the influence of alcohol or various other substances, such as drugs, but it is not doing any good if it is an addiction. Raising your tone at a person who is bothering you can be a relief, but it does not help your relationship with that person nor how you feel about yourself. It may feel good to spend a lot of time-consuming adult content, gambling your savings away, or video games for a few hours, but if this has taken up most of your life, then you will feel empty and ashamed.

· · ·

A better way to feel good is to make choices that are good for you in the long run. And making these decisions requires some skill. In a sense, it is similar to responding to your emotions and impulses with self-awareness by telling yourself, for example, "I am the one in charge of this ship," in many ways. This is what controlling your emotions and impulses means.

Fundamentally, controlling your emotions and impulses is about intentionally reducing or increasing the intensity of emotions and deciding whether to act on impulse or desire. Some much-needed skills for becoming better at managing your emotions and impulses are:

- Being able to determine and control where your attention is focused.
- When something is "happening," decide and control when and how much attention is focused on different aspects of the situation, including your thoughts, feelings, and impulses.
- Choose how you see your emotional reaction to things.
- Avoid acting on wishes or wishes.
- When you are angry, anxious, scared,

addicted, etc., imagine and do things that calm you down.

This may seem like a lot at first, and you may be even overthinking all of this instead of learning from it. But they are skills that we can all learn when we are ready, in our own way, at our own pace.

A key skill is stepping back from a situation and reflecting on your thoughts, feelings, and things you want to do. This includes remembering your values and goals and what is really important in this situation and/or relationship. If you can observe your reactions and think about them as they occur, you have more control over your feelings, thoughts, and behaviors. You open the door to making decisions, not just reacting.

Emotional awareness is another key. It is important to understand how you feel, especially when you have complex emotions (such as sadness, anger, shame, and resentment). Without this awareness, you are in an "autonomous driving" state, driven by old habits. But if you are emotionally aware, you can realize what happening before it is too late. You can truly control your response. You can make the right decision and make you feel good in the future.

.   .   .

What are the requirements of these forms? There are impulses that appear suddenly and can act automatically. Familiar but painful emotions, such as sadness, fear, and shame, can last for minutes, hours, or days. Over time, desires become more and more difficult to resist, even if only to escape stress and anxiety. The ability to regulate emotions and impulses is first developed in childhood since we were babies. We learn (or do not learn) in interpersonal relationships, especially relationships with parents and other caregivers.

First, these adults provide examples of people who can (or can not) be aware of their emotions. People who can (or can not) express their feelings in beneficial but not hurtful words. People who can (or can not) tolerate bad emotions without impulsively showing them or avoiding them due to alcohol, drugs, or other addictions.

Second, parents and caregivers with good self-regulation skills provide a safe and comfortable relationship, allowing children to gradually develop emotional awareness, tolerance for unwanted feelings, and control of harmful impulses. Ideally, caring adults will provide children with the support and acceptance they need to learn to regulate emotions and impulse skills.

When children are neglected, exploited, or abused by their caregivers, they experience extreme emotions such as fear, shame, and anger. Unfortunately, they do not have the support of adults to deal with these emotions and the destructive impulses that follow.

Parents and caregivers have several restrictions in this regard. There are many different situations, including parents neglecting, emotionally, physically, or sexually abusing their children; loving parents but overwhelmed by stress and addiction (due to their poor self-regulation ability), and usually excellent but somehow Caregivers who cannot identify or deal with children's problems and have had unwanted or abusive sexual experiences.

You can find examples in your own life to see where your self-regulation ability is the strongest and the weakest. Generally speaking. However, men who have had unwanted or abusive sexual experiences in childhood have difficulty regulating their emotions and impulses.

It is mainly about motivation, focus, discipline, and practice. Healing from the effects of what is happening, especially initially, usually means a lot of work to develop skills to regulate emotions and impulses. In addition, because men are taught to pay attention to certain emotions rather than others and act on certain impulses rather than others, they rarely get rid of the typical male difficulties regulating emotions and impulses.

.   .   .

Learning and strengthening self-regulation skills is not rocket science. This is mainly about being motivated, focused, and trained (enough) to practice, practice, and practice more. We all have our own "weaknesses," where it is difficult for us to regulate our emotions and impulses. Therefore, it takes time, effort, and a lot of practice to retrain yourself to respond healthily to those challenging situations and feelings.

3.2 The side-effects of negative thinking and how to overcome it

You think illness is the cause of your body's fatigue or long-term pain, but have you ever thought that negative thoughts could be the cause? Pessimism is known to affect more than just your emotional health. In fact, doctors have found that compared to people with a positive attitude, people with many negative emotions are more likely to suffer from degenerative brain diseases, cardiovascular problems, and digestive problems and recover much more slowly from the disease.

Negative emotions are often the product of depression or insecurity. It can be due to illnesses, life events, personality problems, and drug abuse. Like many things in life, negative emotions can become a habit. Occurrences such as regular and consistent criticism, deeply distrustful thoughts, and personal contradictions create neural pathways in the brain that promote sadness. These negative tendencies can cause our brains to distort the facts, making it more difficult to break the negative cycle. Fortunately, most habits can be broken. Experts say it takes 21 days to get rid of a habit.

It is widely known that negativity can manifest in a myriad of ways. Some of those ways are:

- Cynicism: The general distrust of people and their motives.
- Hostility: Hostility towards others; unwillingness to develop relationships.
- Filtering: Only noticing what should be a pleasant experience or bad memory in memory.
- Polarized thinking: thinking that if something or someone is not perfect, then it must be terrible.
- Draw a conclusion: Assume that something bad will happen due to the current situation.
- Disaster theory: Believe that disasters are inevitable.
- Blame: Blame others for personal illnesses and victims of uncontrollable events in life.
- Emotional reasoning: Use your emotions to define what is true and what is not.

- Change fallacy: think that if people or the environment change, you will be happy.
- Heaven's reward fallacy: a negative assumption that hard work and sacrifice will always be rewarded. When the reward does not come, you will be in pain and frustrated.

Negative thoughts and emotions are natural responses to disasters and pain. But long-term negative emotions can cause serious health problems. Negative emotions put our body in a stressful or "fight or flight" mode. Our body aims to respond to stressful situations by releasing cortisol into the blood, making you more alert and focused. Although some stress is good for us, too much can be harmful to our health. Prolonged negative emotions slow down digestion and reduce the ability of the immune system to fight inflammation. This is why negative people are more likely to get sick than optimistic people. Some of the more common physical manifestations of negative thoughts are:

- Headache
- Chest pain
- Fatigue
- Upset stomach

- Sleep problems
- Anxiety
- Depression
- Social withdrawal
- Dramatic changes in metabolism (i.e., overeating or under-eating, which can also harm your health)
- Smoking or substance abuse is more likely to be used as a coping method

One of the most common ways to deal with negative thoughts is to attempt to replace them with positive thoughts which make you feel better.. Suppose you just learned that you have a health problem. You may tell yourself, "My life will no longer be the same" or "This is the beginning of my end." There is a chance that this will severely weaken your body, especially canceled when you need it to be strong". Hence, you may only deteriorate your health further by having these kinds of intrusive and negative thoughts.

Instead, try saying something like: "This will be a challenge for a while, but if I have patience, I can learn to adjust and still enjoy my life" or "This is a setback for me, but I can surely recover from it." This kind of thinking will make you feel better and more hopeful, and it also helps your body.

Do you have negative thoughts now? Take a moment, listen to your thoughts, and watch to see if you do. If what you say to yourself makes you feel bad, remember: you are responsible for what you say. So why not think about something more encouraging?

Because the mind and body are connected, your thoughts will affect your health. By saying more inspiring things to yourself, you are telling your brain to make chemicals that can lower blood pressure, reduce your risk of heart disease, strengthen your immune system to fight infection and disease, reduce your stress level and make you feel less anxious, help you avoid stomach problems, insomnia and back pain, make you happier and more optimistic about the future.

Sometimes negative thoughts are related to your daily lifestyle. So here are some things you can try now to help you see the bright side of life:

Focus on how you feel now. If you are sad, feel sad. But do not tell yourself that you have always felt this way, and you are destined to be sad forever. The sadness passed. A negative thought will persist ... until you let it go.

Share your feelings with people close to you. Everyone has negative thoughts from time to time. Talking about it with other people can help you put these ideas into perspective.

Do something nice for yourself. Maybe you can work less today and play more with your children. Or you can find something that makes you laugh.

Take a moment to count your blessings. Each of us has many things to be thankful for. What do you admire?

Eat well. Sleep well. Be positive. The better you treat your body, the better it will feel.

3.3 The basics of a productive mindset and how to be more productive

Productivity is a common goal we all strive for. Do our best, show ourselves, be authentic and make the most of the time we have. But what happens when our day is affected by unforeseen external factors. Or are we mentally ill? What happens when our daily life is inter-rupted, and our intention to do things is destroyed? We will now talk about some ways of obtaining a productive mindset.

Make sure to be prepared at all times. Imagine a meeting was canceled, or a friend is late. The entire plan you made ahead of time must be rearranged at that very moment. When that moment appeared on our schedule, we suddenly had time that we did not have before. Instead of wasting this time in disgust or disappointment, it is better to take advantage of this time. Treat it as a gift instead of a waste. The "freed up" time can be used to do things, like write a "thank you" or "I noticed" card to share your gratitude with the people you work with. You can also use this time to update your "to do" list. You can even read a chapter from a book or make some calls that have been put off. When you give up the things you can not control and focus on the things you can control, you will take a big step towards getting your day back on track.

Inhale. Exhale. But do not forget to breathe in again. Sometimes we are so obsessed with what happens at the moment that we even forget to breathe. When unforeseen circumstances arise, stress is a natural response. Remember that deep breathing can calm busy times and allow you to refocus on where you want this day to come. This kind of reflective pause helps us focus better and increase energy. Relaxed bodies are also more confident, which is exactly what they need when things seem out of control. Pause. Reflect. Refocus.

"Do this. Do that. Do not forget to drink that, and do not forget the milk!". This all refers to being present mentally. A list of reminders constantly made in our mind every day allows us to live in the future and remember the good and the bad; we live in the past. When we are always in the future or the past, we will miss the beauty of the present. Have you ever talked to someone who does not seem to accept what you are saying? Maybe they are daydreaming or not interested, but more often, they think about things in the future or remember things that happened in the past, maybe even in an hour. No matter what keeps you from concentrating on your conversation, I bet it does not feel good to stand on your distracted recipient. Do not be that person. Attend. Fully participate in whatever you are doing to ensure your best work and high-quality productivity.

If you want to experience the best, you have to work hard. This also means that taking care of yourself is important, as you should not burn out. We all have people tell us that we need to get enough sleep every night, and we should never skip breakfast, right? But what about the 24 hours in between? To create a more productive way of thinking for ourselves, we must learn to control ourselves throughout the day. Do you need caffeine? Do you need to get up and dance or do some jumping exercises to get the blood to flow? Do you need to breathe fresh air? Experiencing what your body desires can make a real difference. Revitalization is not only good for productivity but also good for the soul.

Productivity means that we are doing what we have said to do in the time we promised. So, review your daily work and develop a mentality to do more; you will accomplish more every day.

With the theoretical part out of the way, we can now move on to how you can become more productive. We will now go over some tips that you can try to implement to increase your productivity and lessen your procrastination!

Use a to-do list

Yes, we are talking about the old school "write everything you need to accomplish" type of to-do list. We recommend that you do it the night before you need to complete the task to save time during the day. When writing your to-do list, be sure to write down all the things you need to complete by a specific date, for example;

- Review of the math exam

- Research for the history test
- Complete the thesis on Monday

However, to further improve your work Efficiency-press, schedule the items on this list every hour, including your daily activities, rest, and time to eat. For example, this will help you to look at each day correctly and stay efficient at your work at its best because you need to complete the "deadline" before a certain time;

8 AM - wake up

9 AM. - review math test

10:30 AM - 10-minute break

10:40 AM - do historical test investigation

12:10 PM - 10-minute break

12:20 PM - 14 Monday late at 14:00 to complete part of your thesis: 50PM - lunch

and so on, until bedtime ...

Then when you complete each task, cross it off your list. In this way, you will be able to visualize your progress, observe the number of tasks you must complete, and reduce the number of tasks. Trust us when we say that if you can remove everything from your list before the day is out, you will feel so successful and satisfied that you will be even more encouraged to continue with the to-do list.

. . .

Figure out how you learn

Everyone has their own way of learning. Some of us find it easier to visualize what we need to learn. Others find it easier to consume information and learn by reading and/or writing things. There is no right or wrong way to learn. In most cases, all students belong to one of these four groups.

- Visual learners

This type of learning is used by people who learn by observing things: diagrams, tables, infographics, etc. This learning method is most suitable for students who remember and consume information by observing things. If this sounds familiar, be sure to start learning visually, as it will help you remember more test facts and information.

- Kinesthetic Learners

This learning method is tailored for people who learn best through experience. This can be anything from actual experiments and tests to practical experience. If you find that you are learning more than doing something to consume and retain knowledge, this may be your way of learning, and you should implement it while studying to increase your productivity.

- Auditory Learners

This learning style is best for people who can better remember information when they hear it out loud. This can be recorded by attending lectures, discussions, or listening to the information, usually orally. If you often find yourself reading aloud to remember more information while studying, you may be an auditory learner.

- Reading and writing

This learning style is relevant for students who retain information better by writing and reading. This can come from textbooks, lecture notes, or information written in textbooks. If you often find yourself taking notes and then revising them, this may be your learning style.

Find the style that suits you best, adjust your learning style and improve your work efficiency. If you find a mix of multiple learning styles, stick with them at the same time. Once you realize your habits and determine a learning style, you will immediately become more efficient because you will retain more information in a shorter period.

Rest adequately

Rest during periods of intense studying is an important part of realizing one's potential. It can also help you stay focused and motivated, and a productive rest should refresh you and prepare you to refocus on learning. This is because our brains can only process a certain amount of information before we start to get tired and lose focus. By pushing our thoughts beyond their capabilities, we will be stressed and start to feel tired.

Therefore it is important to take breaks during your work or responsibilities to ensure that your work efficiency, concentration, and energy are maintained at the optimal level because you need to consume a lot of information every day.

Although there is no fixed time frame for rest, because everyone has a different timetable and method that best suits them, it is important to include rest time throughout the day. The Pomodoro Technique teaches us to work or study for 25 minutes and then take a 5-minute break to ensure that our attention is at its best. However, you can increase or decrease these periods to suit your work plan and see which period suits you best.

No matter how long you choose to rest, be sure to use this time to do something completely different from your studies. Maybe go for a walk, talk with friends, or check out your favorite social media platforms. This will give you a break and improve the efficiency of your work when you return to study.

. . .

Treat and reward yourself when you accomplish something.

We strongly believe in the importance of recognizing success and celebrating achievement. With this in mind, it is important to reward yourself for your hard work. The reward system will provide you with additional motivation and help you stay focused and get through every day efficiently to finally earn rewards.

So every time you complete a challenging task, review day or week, or complete that work, reward yourself. It doesn't matter what size you think is appropriate. This can be anything from listening to your favorite podcast, watching a movie, or having coffee with friends.

After completing certain tasks, a small rewards-related stimulus will motivate you to move on and complete the task. The reward system can play a big role in your overall productivity - who doesn't like to do what they love after a productive day? We know we do this... so go ahead and be kind to yourself... you've earned it!

Achieving more goals in a shorter period is not to extend work hours but to work smarter and more effectively, not just to be efficient.

Some people are very efficient, know how to

complete tasks, and always check things on their to-do lists. These people are very busy, but they are not always the most efficient.

On the other hand, there are also highly effective people. These people are also very efficient, but they take their efforts to the next level by focusing first on completing the tasks that greatly impact their lives. This means that they are very efficient at work and can do the right things instead of being busy with many unimportant tasks.

The process of achieving more goals in less time is not always easy, but it is very simple.

First, you must start with your goal. If your goals are long-term goals, you need to make sure that your short-term goals support them. By setting your goals first, you can focus on the most important and productive things throughout the day to achieve those goals. When you care about what you need to achieve and what you need to achieve your goals, it will be much easier to stay focused and increase productivity.

Once your goals are set, you must believe that you can actually achieve them. Hard work, well, hard work, but worth it, so your success depends on your self-confidence. You must recognize the fact that to get where you want, you must keep trying and trying. As long as you do this, you will succeed in the end.

Why? Because you can take full control of your life.

Yes, luck and some external forces started to work, but in the end, you did it. So it's up to you to do it or not. In addition, don't forget that in the process of working hard to achieve your goals, you will find new opportunities and different options. Don't be afraid to take advantage of them.

Highly effective people focus on their tasks, but they also spend time trying new things, trying new methods, and reaping the rewards. By doing this, you can also optimize your work efficiency by keeping your eyes open to understand new things to learn and do.

However, with this in mind, it is also important to focus on one goal at a time. Trying to achieve too many goals at the same time will all be halfway there. It is best to focus on one thing at a time and do that very well before moving on to the next.

Another thing highly effective people understand is how to ask for help and know that they need help. Do you want to be efficient? Be with people who trust you, inspire you, and inspire you, and these people, in turn, are inspired by you. Even if you don't achieve all of your goals, your life will be infinitely rich.

. . .

By remembering these points, you will be able to do in-time (remember that Rome was not built in a day...) do more work in less time because you will understand the basic value of achieving this goal. So put all the above skills in focus and start reaching your goals.

FOUR

BOOSTING YOUR PROBLEM-SOLVING SKILLS

Problem-solving skills can help you solve problems quickly and effectively. This is one of the key skills that employers look for among job applicants because employees with these skills tend to be self-sufficient. Problem-solving skills require quick identification of potential problems and implementation of solutions.

Problem-solving is considered a soft skill (or personal advantage), not a difficult skill learned through education or training. You can improve your problem-solving skills by becoming familiar with common problems in the industry and learning from more experienced employees.

Troubleshooting begins with identifying the problem. For example, teachers may need to figure out how to improve student performance on writing proficiency tests. To do this, the teacher will review the writing test and look for areas for improvement. You can see that students can construct simple sentences, but they work hard to write paragraphs and organize them in an essay. To solve this problem, the teacher and students will study the writing style and timing of compound sentences, write paragraphs, and organize an essay.

4.1 Understanding effective problem-solving: what is it?

Being a human being with an organized life does not mean you do not have problems. Rather, it means that you know how to resolve problems when they arise effectively. Unfortunately, there are many examples of people who are promoted to managerial or leadership positions because they are capable and good at the technical skills required to complete the job. These people suddenly discover that they need to "think independently" and solve more advanced and complex problems than they needed to tackle before. To tackle a problem, there are several steps one can follow to do so:

Step 1: Identify the problem

"How are things when they are what we want?" This question can help you find the standard by which we measure where we are now. If things go the way we want, what will it be like? If this person is doing what we want him to do, what will he do? Then ask this important question: How much deviation from the norm can be tolerated? This is the problem. From an engineering point of view, your tolerance may be small. From a behavioral perspective, you may have more tolerance. When this person does not do exactly what I told them to do, they can say, "I am fine because I can accept their freedom in this matter." You may need a few other questions for 100% compliance.

Step 2: Analyze the problem

At what stage is this problem? This helps you determine the urgency of the problem, which is usually divided into three stages. The emerging stage is where the problem has just started. It does not pose a direct threat to the way companies operate every day. It has just begun to happen, and you have time to correct it without causing too much damage to the process that it affects.

The mature stage is that this problem causes more than minor damage. It has caused a certain degree of damage. It is necessary to jump on it immediately to repair it so that it does not become a problem. If we do not quickly solve this problem, the consequences may be greater, deeper, and more expensive.

The third stage is the crisis stage, and the problem is so serious that it must be corrected immediately. At this stage, the processes, reputation, finances, etc., of your business have actually been damaged, potentially having a long-term impact on your business capabilities.

. . .

Step 3: Describe the problem

Assuming that the problem is not a complex scientific problem, you should describe the problem in sentence form, and it should be described in 12 or fewer words. In this way, you will know where the problem is. You might then try to distribute it to your team to make sure they agree that this is the source of the problem, it makes sense, and everyone working on the solution is working towards the same goal.

When describing your problem, the most important question is: Are your premises correct? Here is an example: We have all heard or read the engineer's "half empty and half full" story. The speaker raised the water glass, asked if the glass was half empty or half full, and then discussed it in the group, usually expecting some optimistic lessons. In this version, an engineer replied in the room: "I see that this glass of water is twice as large as you need."

You see, sometimes, when you are responsible for the problem and trying to establish the premise of the problem, you tend to look at it from your perspective. However, the premise may be inaccurate, or you may just need another perspective to view it. If your premise is wrong, or at least incomplete, then you have not fully understood the problem and have not considered the best options for the solution.

.   .   .

Step 4: Find the Root Cause

This step involves asking and answering many questions. Ask the following questions: What caused this problem? Who is responsible for this problem? When did this problem first appear? Why is this happening? How did this change in standards come about? Where is the most painful? How do we proceed to solve this problem?

In addition, ask the most important question: Can we solve this problem forever so that it does not happen again? Because an important aspect of leadership is finding solutions that people can benefit from in the long run without having to deal with the same problems repeatedly.

Step 5: Develop a workaround

Almost all the problems you have to deal with have more solutions than the first problem you think of. Therefore, it is best to develop a list of workarounds so that you and your team can evaluate and decide which method is best for a particular problem. A rule often used is the "⅓ + 1" rule to reach a consensus around one of the first two or three solutions, which is the best for every participant. Then rank these solutions based on efficiency, cost, long-term value, resources you have, and solutions you can work on to solve the problem. Then, take a closer look at each of these solutions and determine which you think is the best solution for this problem at this point.

Step 6: Implement the Solution

Implementing the solution of your choice may include developing an implementation plan. It can also include planning for what happens next if the solution goes wrong and the solution does not work the way you envisioned it. Implementation means that all members of your team know and understand their role in making the solution work. There is a timeline for execution. You have a system to track whether the solution fixes the problem.

Step 7: Measure results

Building on the implementation plan in Step 6, be sure to track and measure results so that you can answer the following questions: Is it effective? Is this a good solution? Did we learn some knowledge that can be applied to other potential problems in the implementation process?

. . .

These seven simple steps will help you become a more effective and efficient problem solver in your organization. As you practice this process and develop skills, these steps will become more natural to you to use them unknowingly.

4.2 Techniques to improve your problem-solving skills

Most people think you must be very smart to be a good problem solver, but this is not the case. You do not need to be smart to solve problems; you need to practice. When you understand the different steps to solve a problem, you can find an excellent solution. In this chapter, we will be reviewing some tips that can help you improve your problem-solving skills.

Try to focus on solutions, not problems. Neuroscientists have shown that if you focus on problems, your brain will not find solutions. The reason behind this is that when you focus on the problem itself, you are feeding the negativity, activating the negative emotions in the brain as a result. These emotions get in the way of possible solutions. We are not implying that you should "ignore the problem," but rather try to stay calm. First, admit that the problem is useful; then turn your attention to a solution-oriented mindset. In this mindset, you can focus on what the "answer" might be, rather than rambling "what is wrong?" and "Whose fault is it?".

Adjust to using the "5 Whys" to define the problem clearly. The 5 Whys is a problem-solving framework that can help you find the source of the problem.

By repeatedly asking the "why" question about the problem, you can get to the root cause of the problem so that you can find the best solution and solve the root of the problem once and for all. It can go deeper than simply asking why five times. For example: If the question is "Always late for work," ask yourself, "Why am I late for work?" Maybe you answered with, "I always click the snooze button; I just want to keep sleeping." Now, ask yourself, "Why should I keep sleeping?" You might answer with, "I feel tired in the morning." A good follow-up question would be, "Why do you feel tired in the morning?" You might answer with, "I slept too late the day before yesterday." Now, ask yourself, "Why did I go to bed late?". Your answer can be anything but imagine you answer with "I am not sleepy after drinking coffee, I just keep browsing my Facebook feed, and somehow I can not stop." Keep asking yourself multiple "why-based" questions to come to the root cause of the problem, to make it easier for yourself to tackle the said problem. A solution for this example would be setting more alarms, avoiding coffee at night, and maybe even set your phone far away, so you do not browse social media late at night.

Try to simplify things—as humans, we tend to make things unnecessarily complicated. Try to simplify your questions by generalizing. Remove all details and return to the source. Try to find a very simple and clear solution; you may be surprised by the results! We all know that the simplest things are often the most effective.

Make sure to list as many solutions as possible - try to find "all possible solutions," even if they seem ridiculous at first. It is important to keep an open mind to encourage creative thinking, which can trigger possible solutions. You might have heard the phrase, "no idea is a bad idea." This phrase often helps in creative thinking, brainstorming, and other problem-solving techniques. Whatever you do, do not make fun of yourself for offering a "stupid solution" because usually crazy ideas trigger other more feasible solutions. Instead, try to change your focus and see things in a new way. For example, you can try to change your goals and find an opposite solution! Even if it feels silly, new and unique methods often inspire new solutions.

．　．　．

Try implementing phrases that imply possibility - use phrases like "what if..." and "imagine if..." to guide your thinking. These terms can open our brains, allow us to think creatively, and encourage program solutions. Avoid closed and negative language, such as "I do not think ..." or "But this is wrong ...".

Try not to view the problem as something "terrible"! - if you consider what the real problem is, it is really just feedback on your current situation. Every problem tells you that something is not currently working, and you need to find a new way to solve it. So try to approach the problem neutrally, without any judgment. Practice focusing on defining the problem, stay calm, and do not overcomplicate.

4.3 Examples of problem-solving in real life

In this chapter, we will go over some more practical, everyday examples of how problem-solving is used to solve various occurrences that may impede your plans, work, or even general well-being. These examples do not have direct solutions listed in them, so look at them as practice examples that you can work on to test how far your problem-solving skills have come!

．　．　．

1. You are stuck in a traffic jam, making you run late for work.

Due to busy schedules and competing demands on time, arriving where needed on time can be a real challenge. When traffic stops, problem-solving techniques can help you find alternative ways to avoid congestion, solve the immediate situation, and develop solutions to avoid this situation in the future.

2. What are the strange stains on the living room carpet?

Parents, pet owners, and spouses have faced this situation. For example, yesterday, the living room carpet was very clean, but for some reason, a mysterious stain appeared, and no one claimed it. To clean it effectively, you must first find out what it is. Troubleshooting can help you find the culprit, diagnose the cause of the stains, and develop an action plan to make your home look new.

3. What does my teenager's room smell like, and why does it smell so odd?

Parents with a lot of problem-solving experience know for a fact that the source of the funky odor is most likely linked to an area either in the closet or somewhere under the bed. The challenge is to figure out how to control and mitigate the impact and develop workable solutions to avoid it in the future.

4. Cars should not be making loud, almost thumping-like noises.

As with many workplace problems, this can be a situation where troubleshooting experts are brought in in the form of your trusted mechanic. However, if this is not an option, problem-solving skills can help diagnose and assess the situation's impact and ensure that you can get where you need it.

5. What could the baby be crying for?

Is it just an incident that can be resolved by changing diapers, breastfeeding, and taking a short nap? Or is there a potential problem that requires further investigation and attention, such as stress, illness, or discomfort? The ability to solve problems is a parent's best friend.

6. My daughter/son has a science project to present tomorrow

Sometimes the challenge is not the impact but the urgency. Problem-solving skills can help you quickly assess the situation and develop an action plan to complete the science project and submit it on time.

7. What gift should I give for my spouse's birthday?

Like many questions, this question may not have an obvious "correct answer" or solution. Now is the time to apply these problem-solving skills to assess the impact of past decisions, combining current environmental cues and available resources to choose the perfect gift that will put a smile on your partner's face.

8. Someone threw away a whole roll of toilet paper, and water accumulated in the bathtub.

Oh, it is time to hurry up. The emergency situation must be resolved to control the impact, determine the cause (who is responsible), and plan of action to get things back to normal. Problem-solving techniques can help you avoid the possibility of panic and expensive cleaning.

9. The deadline for submitting the proposal has been advanced for this afternoon!

You have been working on that great proposal for several weeks, until the last three days, when you received a call saying that the deadline was pushed forward until today. Troubleshooting techniques can help you determine if you can meet the new deadlines and how your methods may need to be changed.

10. What is the plan for dinner?

Whether you plan to eat alone, with your family, or entertain friends and colleagues, meal planning can be a source of your daily stress. The application of problem-solving skills can correctly view the dilemma of dinner, help put food on the table and make everyone happy.

FIVE

EFFICIENT DECISION-MAKING TO IMPROVE YOUR LIFE

Decisions are more or less a personal trait, but effective decision-making is a skill that can be learned and improved like any other skill. This is our effective decision-making guide to help you at home and work.

We make decisions every day; You will not even be aware of most of them, but high-risk decisions are often stressful and can take a long time. That is why effective decision-making can mean the difference between success or failure. Understanding the decision-making framework can significantly impact your career, personal life, and overall stress level.

Whether as a professional in a company or your private and personal life, we are always making decisions. Although these options may look very different at first glance, they do have some similarities in how we decide how to deal with them.

Business decisions

Starting from the concept of an enterprise, a decision must be made; what is the nature of the business, who is the target customer, and where should the business be located? These are just a few examples that show that making a decision can have a lasting impact, so it needs to be considered thoroughly. This reflects important personal decisions, such as where to live and what job or career path to choose. The way we handle these decisions can be just as complicated and complex. As your career unfolds, the kinds of decisions you make will be riskier and have a greater impact on more people, so you make the right decision and make sure you have the right information to do so. The reason for being so important.

Personal Decision Making

Personal decision-making is just as important as business decision-making but generally involves far fewer people. However, because they involve the people closest to us and our private lives, they are generally more influential than some of the business decisions we make. Ultimately, they determine who we are, who we are closest to, and our priorities in life. Your personal decision includes everything from what to have lunch to get married to and where to live.

Consumer decision making

Consumer decision-making can be made in a personal or business setting; It covers everything from what type of milk you like to deciding which supplier to work with on the project. Like business and personal decision-making, you have your own set of factors and considerations that need to be balanced, such as budget and budget. Quality and several unknowns when buying from a newcomer.

5.1 What are decision-making skills, and why are they useful?

Decision-making skills show that you can choose between two or more alternatives. Once you have processed all the available information and talked to the appropriate point of contact involved in a particular situation, you can make a decision. Generally speaking, it is important to identify the processes that will help you make the right decisions on your organization's behalf and work together to identify biases that may affect your organization's results. Listed below will be some areas in life in which decision-making skills are commonly used.

· · ·

Problem Solving

Leaders can use their problem-solving skills to make critical decisions for their businesses. You must consider different perspectives to consider the many variables required to make a well-thought-out decision. You must separate emotions from your conversations with people who will influence your decision. The essence of having problem-solving skills is that you can make decisions quickly and efficiently, so you need to research and pay close attention to details to match the facts with the situation you are solving.

Leadership

Leadership is defined as the behavior of organizing multiple employees within an organization. Good leadership can reach a consensus on specific decisions. In this case, leadership involves evaluating the status quo with people and motivating them to achieve goals after making a decision.

Make sure you take the time to build strong relationships with your colleagues so that you can get to know them and make them feel comfortable talking freely around you. The more loyal and personable you are, the more likely you are to work closely with the team and make productive decisions with long-term impact.

. . .

Reasoning

Reasoning is one of the main skills necessary to understand the decisions you can make. Be sure to review all the pros and cons of the decision you are considering taking action for. This is the best way to stay objective and down to earth in this process to reason about the present and plan for the future.

Consider all available and relevant data points to help guide your decision-making and take a stand on who you are making the decision with. You want to align your reasoning with the people you trust and commit to achieving what you are trying to achieve.

Intuition

Intuition is about deciding and trusting your intuition. Your intuition comes from the experiences you have witnessed in the past and the core values that drive you forward every day. The sum of your experience and the lessons you learn from it will influence your decision. You need to connect your intuition with the potential actions you can take and see if your decision is logical and actionable.

Teamwork

You have to work with your colleagues at some point

to make the right decision. For example, you may need to work with your marketing manager to best work with clients and improve last quarter's marketing campaign results.

Here, you use reasoning to break down the options to help customers improve their activities so that the status report can provide you with relevant data. After that, you can weigh the possible key performance indicators (KPIs) to measure your future success. In general, your ability to work with the team determines the results you get and the number of people affected by the team's decision.

Emotional Intelligence

Emotional Intelligence makes you critically aware of your emotions and can express them in a way that encourages action. Your emotions should set the inspiration for your specific career or mission. However, analyzing the data on the topic will determine how well you are informed to make the final decision.

Creativity

Your creativity uses your logical and emotional thinking to produce a unique solution. You need to have trusted employees in your organization to brainstorm for short-term and long-term solutions. You can also use your creativity to arrange conversations with employees during the meeting and the time allocated to ensure that everyone's voice is heard. Consider holding a brainstorming meeting every week to maximize the creativity of your employees to get noteworthy opinions.

Time management

Since decisions must be made quickly, you must describe the time required to make a decision. You always have to work in your situation, but time management allows you to organize how to make decisions. If you must make a decision before the end of the week, you can spend time at each stage of the decision-making process, including possible actions you can take and suggested solutions.

Organization

Organization is critical to making the final decision. You should use this skill to determine the result you are looking for and whether it is the top priority. If you are going to conduct a survey of your product, your first task is to get feedback from your target audience and see if your marketing campaign uses the right people.

. . .

5.2 How to make decisions like a pro: Characteristics and examples of effective decision-making

Efficient decision-making usually revolves around seven generalized steps, regardless of the context or type of decision. The time and focus for each situation will vary from situation to situation. A direct example will follow up each step to showcase the aim of the step and how it should be implemented.

Step 1: Recognize the need to make a decision.

Example: You want to organize a celebration dinner for your friend's birthday.

Step 2: Research information related to decision-making.

Example: Consider the places your friends have mentioned in the past, their dietary needs, and where they like to eat. You will also seek advice from some mutual friends and perhaps check out websites of various places that match your needs.

Step 3: Build multiple solutions.

Example: You have a list of options from the previous exercise.

.   .   .

Step 4: Evaluate each solution.

Example: Some of your mutual friends have dietary requirements, which eliminates some options. Other options may be too far and inconvenient or too expensive to meet everyone's budget.

Step 5: Choose a solution.

Example: After eliminating most of your options by doing this, a friend may tell you that one of the remaining options has a good atmosphere, or it may be close to one of your favorite bars, and make a decision that is in your favor.

Step 6: Implement the decision.

Example: Reserve a table for you and your friends at the restaurant of your choice.

Step 7: Observe the results and review them.

Example: While you are there, you will learn about your friends' reactions, the food, and the overall success of the night. This information can help you make similar decisions in the future.

In cases where multiple solutions cannot be tested, steps 2, 3, and 4 (investigation, generation, and evaluation) must be very careful and time-consuming to minimize risk. This may include lengthy submission processes or bidding exercises for jobs or lengthy collection of information to ensure that you make decisions based on the best data.

Effective decision-making skills can help you effectively complete all stages of the decision-making process. This means providing powerful solutions based on information gathering and proper and fair evaluation of these solutions. Many decision-making techniques can be used, and it is best to try a few of them and see which one is best for you. Below, several different techniques will be mentioned, so make sure to read through all of them and see which one would fit you the best.

Affinity graphs are used to group data based on their interrelationships. The purpose of this technique is to help you understand a lot of information. The process is simple: write down each thought and group-related thoughts. This allows you to group or group ideas and then remove overlaps or see which area is the most popular/populated.

. . .

Cost/benefit analysis is a methodical process that estimates the pros and cons of a decision to achieve the most profitable results. You can use it to mitigate the negative impact of decision-making or in the process of deciding to do or not to do something based on positive results and risks.

The decision tree is a simple and effective model, similar to a flow chart, used to visualize decisions and their consequences.

Heuristics solve problems by creating "good enough" estimates and decisions. This is a flexible way to make decisions quickly, but not as precise or detailed as other decision models, but it is effective in certain situations. For example, if "A" did not work last time, it is unlikely it will work this time, so let us decide to use decision "B."

Influence diagrams, known as ID, can be used to see how two or more factors influence each other. Influence diagrams can include feedback loops. Although simple, they are a great way to understand how multiple factors interact.

. . .

Multi-Criteria Decision Analysis (MCDA) is often the preferred technique for making complex decisions. MCDA decomposes the problem into sub-problems to facilitate analysis and obtain meaningful solutions. An example of this is the analytic hierarchy process, also known as AHP. This method uses mathematics and psychology to organize and analyze complex decisions. The method consists of deconstructing the main problems into smaller problems that are easier to understand and then organizing them in a hierarchical structure according to various aspects such as comprehension, tangibility, or priority.

Multi voting is best used with brainstorming or affinity mapping and is ideal for group decision-making. The team will vote on the ideas generated to achieve team consensus. Trial and error, however, is the least analytical method in making decisions. It is quite rare in business, although it is more likely to happen in people's personal lives. Essentially, you try something, and if it does not work, you try other things until it works. An example of the trial and error method used in the business is using judges from product testing teams. The analysis of which product works best should be able to accurately determine which product to market.

5.3 How to develop your decision-making skills faster and better

No matter how rich your knowledge is, there is always room for improvement. Fortunately, there are many ways to make more effective and efficient decisions at home and in the workplace.

Learning from experience is probably the most common way to improve decision-making ability and, in some respects, the most passive way. Learn from your mistakes and find out through trial and error which methods are effective and which are ineffective. It seems a bit counterintuitive in the short term, but in the long term, nothing can improve your decision-making skills more effectively than learning from experience. However, for this method to be successful, you need to investigate why your decision is valid or invalid and logically consider your actions.

If you prefer to actively improve your decision-making skills and ideally see results faster, there are many options for you to choose from. You can review your standard decision-making process and decide to try the new things in the above list; it can help you better review your choices or make more thoughtful and rational decisions.

Review your information gathering process-the quality of a decision depends on the information on which it is based. Especially at work, we have various data types and information sources available; expanding and improving the way you obtain information will help you make better decisions.

Seek advice from people who are good at decision-making, and ask them to explain their information collection process and strategy, which may differ from yours.

Take courses in key areas such as critical thinking, risk analysis, data analysis, decision-making, and problem-solving, all of which will help your decision-making skills.

A good exercise is to look at your recent decisions; you want to make a different decision. First, keep track of these seven stages and how you completed them for the first time, and how you will now use new information and after-the-fact benefits to change it. Then, when you make another decision in the future, try to apply the second framework.

Decision-making skills can be divided into four main types; problem-solving, collaboration, emotional intelligence, and logical reasoning. However, creativity and strong communication are often very valuable in the decision-making process. The balance of these skills depends on the type of decision you are making and what type of decision it is. For example, you may not need to collaborate too much on personal decision-making, but it is essential in a work or team environment.

Active listening, interpersonal skills, and leadership are some of the most important skills that leaders can have in collective decision-making. The outstanding qualities that need to be demonstrated as a leader are honesty and integrity, trust, ability to motivate others, commitment, and passion, communication, responsibility, empowerment and authorization, creativity and innovation, empathy, resilience, emotional intelligence, humility, transparency, vision, and goals... Combining all of these qualities and using them to lead your team will definitely help you make great decisions.

To help you solve problems, seek critical thinking, analysis, and logic skills. These are particularly valuable in steps 4 and 7 of the decision-making process. Whether it is group work or individual work, good time management is essential to reduce the pressure that can lead to wrong decisions.

Strategic decision-making is the process of making decisions based on broader and often longer-term objectives. This is very common in business and will guide decisions based on company goals or indicators. Lateral thinking is a particularly useful problem-solving skill because the problem solver must often consider hypothetical situations that have not yet occurred. An example of a strategic decision is whether a company wants to become the most popular chocolate bar brand.

Strategic decisions are divided into tactical decisions to achieve this objective: if the strategy is considered long-term, the tactics are medium-term. In the case of a chocolate bar company, the tactical decision might be to improve the formula or change the packaging design. They can also make a tactical decision not to develop new candy or cake shapes, as this will distract them from the candy bar task.

The decomposition of tactical decisions into operational decisions allows the company to make day-to-day short-term decisions effectively. For example, the chocolate bar company decided to change the packaging. The operational decision may be which team members are best suited for the project.

Strategic decisions are not limited to companies. For example, suppose you want to save money. In that case, the only way to achieve this goal is to make a series of smaller decisions, avoid buying expensive items, eat at home rather than take out, and ultimately save enough money to achieve your goal.

Learning to make effective decisions is one thing, but how to show effective decisions? You must do this at all stages of your career, from interviews to reviews. Here are some tips to demonstrate your decision-making skills:

If you are evaluating various options, make sure others know what the criteria are and how you evaluate them so that others can understand that your decision-making is a process and how Just a quick guess.

In many cases, data-driven decision-making is synonymous with logical or rational decision-making.

Generally speaking, the best way to demonstrate skills is to communicate well throughout the usage process. Make sure others understand the decision and the factors that influenced it.

Make sure to review your decision - If you do not review it later, you will not know if your decision was correct. For important decisions (like vendors), you may want to set up regular reviews to do this. A good decision after six months may not be a good decision after 18 months.

SIX

IMPROVING YOUR REASONING

Logical reasoning is a critical and rational way of thinking and solving problems. Improving decision-making skills is as important as becoming a digital or text writer. Reasoning is a separate part of many entrance exams, including JEE, CAT, and UPSC. In addition, people with good reasoning skills have achieved more in life than others.

Logical reasoning is a way of rational and critical thinking and problem-solving. Improving decision-making skills is as important as becoming a digital or text writer. This process requires a series of systematic steps based on rational explanation and mental calculation. Reasoning is a separate part of many entrance exams, including JEE, CAT, and UPSC. In addition, people with good reasoning skills have achieved more in life than others.

. . .

To improve logical reasoning ability, candidates must first optimize their observation ability. Once you can observe the situation, it becomes very easy to understand the real context through correct inferences. Thus, it can enhance a person's pattern and trend analysis skills. If you follow a systematic approach and invest at least three months a day, it is not difficult to decode patterns and structures more accurately and solve syllogism problems.

Unlike any other field, logical reasoning also has a set of terms that you must be familiar with, such as premises, hypotheses, conclusions, arguments, observations, reasoning, and various types of statements. Familiarity with all of these is necessary to understand the concept of learning in logical reasoning.

There is no additional practice in logical reasoning. The variable nature of the problem makes it difficult to find a set of rules or methods. Although some formulas can be calculated to solve these problems, most problems require a unique approach. Therefore, to achieve proficiency and perfection, candidates must solve various problems every day. Keep in mind the time frame; you need to gradually increase the speed of problem-solving every minute. Therefore, in all competitive exams where reasoning plays a key role, time management is an extremely important success factor.

Logical reasoning, critical thinking, and problem-solving skills are part of a set of meta-skills that can increase the candidate's IQ and greatly improve analytical skills. By responding to various analytical and digital challenges, being prepared can also build self-esteem and resilience. This quality improves judgment and helps achieve the goals of interpersonal relationships that later became leadership traits. Logical thinking is an essential feature of smart engineers, managers, and other executives in the business world. The lack of this indispensable personality attribute will lead to failure in exams and the workplace.

Remember, if it is fun, learning will pay off. Since the first civilization, games have been an important part of the general development of students. In addition to refreshing, games are also believed to help apply logic when performing tasks. Therefore, a person should be good at games with great logic or problem-solving elements, such as chess or Sudoku crosswords, word search, brainteasers, brainteasers. These games can stimulate the player's cognition and create sensual organs, and help the mind. Curious ideas, the premise of logical learning.

There are many reasons for mastering logical reasoning, critical thinking, and problem-solving skills to be scored in ability tests, such as JEE, SAT, GMAT, and various other ability tests. These involve a considerable level of competence and commitment. Logical reasoning makes people confident, confident, and firm. Moreover, when one person uses reliable reasons and logic to verify their opinions and arguments, the entire team likes to respect and implement decisions.

The most important thing is that logical thinking can help solve many problems in the workplace, even if these problems are not directly related to an individual's work profile. Many times, professionals who use logical reasoning in the workplace are rarely affected by mental stress and dissatisfaction. They continue to work hard until the desired result is achieved.

6.1 What are the characteristics of logical thinking

When people hear "logical thinking," they generally assume they are lawyers, mathematicians, philosophers, and doctors. That is not bad; it is just incomplete. Logical thinking is a basic skill that we use every day. From waking up in the morning to falling asleep at night, we all use our logical thinking skills. Logic comes from the Greek logos, which means "thought" or "reason." Many of our decisions and thought processes are based on logic. So much so that you may not even realize that you are currently using logical thinking. Driving to work, grocery shopping, buying new appliances, or solving smaller problems all involve logical thinking skills.

Logical thinking is the process of observing, analyzing, and drawing conclusions based on these inferences. In simple terms, logical thinking is using facts and evidence to draw conclusions or solutions; it is the simultaneous use of logic and reasoning in your thinking process.

Logic is commonly defined as "the science dealing with the principles and validity criteria of reasoning and proof: the science of formal principles of reasoning" or as "a way of thinking or explaining something." We can define logical thinking as the act of using logic in a person's thinking process. Of course, this is very simple. But it did not answer this question.

There are many different types of logic and logical thinking, including:

- Formal logic. We generally think of formal logic as a more "traditional" type of logic. Sometimes called philosophical logic, it relates to logic based on the informal setting of the discussion.
- Informal logic. Similar to formal logic, informal logic is the use of logic and formal settings or in everyday settings.
- Mathematical logic. This is a subfield of mathematics that focuses on formal logic because it is related to mathematical applications.
- Reasoning. This is a process of inferring logical conclusions based on premises rather than explicit statements. Inference is to make inferences or draw conclusions based on evidence and reasoning.
- Inductive reasoning. This falls under logical thinking processes that form generalizations based on specific observations known to be true or false.
- Deductive reasoning. Use formal logic to prove or refute a theory. Start with a theory

or hypothesis and try to support your observations. Think of Sherlock Holmes or a scientist. Better understand deductive reasoning.

- Abductive reasoning. Similar to deductive reasoning, abductive reasoning aims to test observations. However, this is generally done in a "bottom-up" direction rather than a deductive "top-down" one.
- Critical thinking. This is the analysis of facts and evidence to form judgments or draw conclusions.

We might think that logical reasoning skills are things that we either have or do not have. Also, although some people may be more inclined to logical thinking, it is a skill that can be learned and improved.

Logical thinking is an essential basic skill. It is used in daily life. We see logical thinking in math, reading comprehension, and daily decision-making. Logical thinking enables you to solve problems, set goals, and reason through decisions. It can even help creative thinking and so on. This skill is important not only for your career but also for your life.

Employers especially look for candidates who demonstrate strong skills after soft skills. Soft skills are different from technical skills, although they have similarities with known transferable skills. They are personal attributes/characteristics or habits, not acquired skills. This is not to say that social skills cannot be learned or strengthened; of course, they can.

Unlike soft skills, hard or technical skills can always be achieved. They are not skills that no one is born with, although some people may be more naturally good at certain skills than others.

Cognitive skills or cognitive functions are the basic skills your brain uses to do almost everything. Without cognitive skills, we cannot process information, hindering us from learning, understanding, retention, or reasoning. Logic and reasoning are part of these basic cognitive skills.

Cognitive abilities have long been considered concrete. Like IQ, we believe that your innate cognitive function will put you in trouble. We are now aware that this is not true. The brain is a muscle like other muscles; cognitive skills can be strengthened through work.

Question everything. You can begin to develop and strengthen your logical thinking skills by questioning everything. Ask yourself why. Stop making assumptions and start reasoning through your decisions and judgments. Check the facts and separate them from the opinions.

When you start asking questions, you can understand things more deeply. You will better understand your thought process and improve your ability to deal with problems of logic and creativity; This skill will help you work more effectively.

Develop the habit of stopping and thinking before acting. If you spend some time thinking about your logical reasoning, you will inevitably strengthen your logic and reasoning skills.

Try to explain the pattern, find the most logical solution, etc. View individual details individually and as part of the whole. Adjust your views and question things deeply, and you will find that you can think more logically without even trying.

Perform logic exercises. The best way to strengthen your muscles is to exercise them. The same applies to skills like logical thinking. There are many ways to integrate logic exercises into your daily life. The more time you spend practicing, the better you will become at using this skill.

Games along the likes of Sudoku and puzzles are a great way to practice logical thinking skills. Many applications also use logic and reasoning. Puzzle games, math games, card games, and word games can improve this skill, not just like work. Riddles and brain teasers can also help you start to think more critically.

If you are looking for more complex logic exercises, consider the free LSAT exercises. Logical and reasoning skills are the foundation of the LSAT; even the writing part requires logical reasoning to explain and respond to prompts.

Try to analyze some logical games in the reasoning part or answer some questions in the logical reasoning part. You can even use the reading comprehension part to help strengthen your logical thinking skills. The reading comprehension exercises in any exam or workbook are sufficient. The

LSAC, the manufacturer of the LSAT, offers free LSAT exams that you can use. You can also do some LSAT exercises for free through the official LSAT preparation program of the LSAC partner Khan Academy.

Expand your horizons. Socializing, building new relationships, and learning new cultures can expand your horizons and develop your logical reasoning skills.

By looking at things from only one (your) angle, you are hurting yourself. When you open your heart to accept different perspectives, you will see different ways of dealing with situations and seeing things.

You may be better able to distinguish facts from opinions (including personal opinions) and handle situations more logically than before.

The ability to see things from all angles is a highly sought-after skill in the workplace. By putting it into practice, you will develop two skills to make you a better candidate for the job.

Be creative. Despite being associated with different brain hemispheres, creative thinking and creative activity can help encourage problem-solving and thus promote logical thinking.

Drawing, learning, or playing a musical instrument and writing are creative ways. However, they are not just activities in the right hemisphere. They all require the use of logic and creativity. By participating in creative activities you like, you can naturally enhance your critical thinking and problem-solving skills.

Music is a language in itself, one that you must learn before you can play any instrument. Writing requires you to think creatively when using language. She uses her imagination and visualization skills while also focusing on facts and linear thinking.

These two activities are firmly embedded in the traditional left-brain and traditional right-brain activities. Although art is only related to creative thinking, you can strengthen your logical thinking skills through these activities.

6.2 How hobbies can enhance your reasoning

Analytical skills are the skills to perform analysis. These skills include the ability to apply logical thinking to break complex problems into component parts. We consciously and unconsciously use analytical skills in many areas of life, such as critical thinking, communication, research, data analysis, and creativity. Analyzing hobbies can be the perfect activity to develop analytical skills.

When we are fully immersed, involved, and absorbed in an activity, our thoughts and behaviors will differ. In positive psychology, this state is called a fluid state, and it is also colloquially referred to as being in a region. In a constantly changing state, we are strongly focused on the present. Our actions and consciousness merge, lose our reflective self-awareness, have a sense of control or personal initiative, and change our subjective experience of time. We experience activities. Your new analytical hobby may be an activity that you need to research in-depth.

Finding a new hobby that you are interested in and like is the best way to improve and improve your skills effectively, easily, and even without worry. Following analytical hobbies can indeed improve your analytical skills. Below you will be able to find some of the more common (or maybe even less common) hobbies you can take up to level up your reasoning.

. . .

Chess

Chess is one of the most popular games in the world, with millions of players participating in local tournaments, international competitions, and private games with friends and family every year. Deciding to learn to play chess has many benefits, one of the main benefits is that you can enjoy interesting and rich new hobbies. Let us take a closer look at how to use chess as a hobby in life.

Playing chess is one of the most valuable hobbies you can bring into life. There are many benefits to playing chess, from practical benefits to cognitive and psychological benefits, and more subtle benefits, such as finding something that does not involve a smartphone or other electronic devices to occupy your time. When you take out chess, you can enjoy the non-technical game time, which is good for your body and mind.

There are many factors to consider when buying a chess set. If you are completely new to chess, your ideal choice is to buy a simple and classic chess set that will not deviate from the traditional Staunton variety used and recognized by most people. On the other hand, if you have played games before or want something different, you can consider choosing interesting variations, such as chess with novel themes or even new things like 3-person chess.

Once you have decided what type of chess you want,

you can start shopping. There are countless chess sets available for purchase today, from low-budget sets that cost less than $15 to luxury sets made of high-quality materials, and the price may be more than $100. This implies that you can invest a lot more for a high-quality experience or invest very little if you feel like you do not need more than the basics.

Playing chess is a good hobby because you can enjoy the game in many different ways. However, the most traditional way to enjoy chess is to play chess with others, which can be done in the following ways:

- Invite friends and family to come to play chess with you
- Contact the chess team and participate in meetings to play chess
- Participate in local tournaments
- Participate in large-scale competitions

If you do not want to play chess directly with others, or there is no such option at the moment, you can play chess on your own! This can be done with electronic chess, or you can manually move the "opposite" pieces according to predetermined moves easily found on the internet.

If you are looking for a fun and rewarding hobby that can help keep you busy while providing you with a host of great benefits, do not wait - start searching for chess now to add to your collection and embrace the hobby of chess.

Solving Rubik's cubes

In the mid-1970s, one of the most cunning riddles was invented, which continued to baffle some of the smartest people in the world. When the Rubik's Cube was first invented and released to the public, almost everyone in North America wanted to see if they could solve the impossible 3D puzzle. Perhaps it is because most people cannot solve the puzzle that the Rubik's Cube is so popular, but the frustration and love for this little toy lasted for about thirty years, and it is still as popular as before. But when is such a simple toy so popular, and why should you be based on it? The simple answer is that the challenge itself is worth your time and effort, but another reason is that solving the puzzle is so simple. This is the beginning of the Rubik's Cube game.

Once you have mastered the basics of riddles, refer to puzzle solving. The next step is to improve the speed of puzzle-solving. The Speed Cube hobby is essentially solving the Rubik's Cube as quickly as possible, and it has a huge following throughout the hobby. For those not interested, most of the appeal lies in the idea of solving impossible cubes at unheard of speed. As beginners level up and improve their skills, it is possible to solve cubes at a ridiculous speed or even with your eyes closed. There is no doubt that the inventor of the Rubik's Cube can never imagine how competitive and fun his simple invention has become.

The Rubik's Cube is a 3D mechanical puzzle. It was once called "The Rubik's Cube" but was later renamed Rubik's Cube and sold by Ideal Toys. In 1980, this puzzle won the German Game of the Year award, and in January 2009, 350 million cubes were sold worldwide. It is one of the best-selling puzzle games in the world and is generally considered the best-selling toy in the world.

In the classic Rubik's Cube, each of the six faces is covered by nine stickers of matching colors, traditionally white, red, blue, orange, green, and yellow. The pivot mechanism allows each face to rotate independently, mixing colors to have multi-color stickers. The problem most people face is that when you move one face, you also move the other face, so the trick is to manipulate these faces to make them group together. To solve this problem, each face must be a solid color again. Now similar puzzles have been made with different sticker numbers instead of all Rubik's Cubes. The original 3 × 3 × 3 versions celebrated their 30th anniversary in 2010.

With the popularity of Rubik's Cube, the market is flooded almost immediately with knock-offs and changes from the original game, which is no wonder. There are many different variants of the Rubik's cube, from the original 3x3x3 cube up to seven layers: 2 × 2 × 2 (pocket / mini cube), standard 3 × 3 × 3 cubes, 4 × 4 × 4 (Rubik's Revenge / Master Cube), And 5 × 5 × 5 (Teacher's Cube), 6 × 6 × 6 (VCube 6) and 7 × 7 × 7 (VCube 7).

CESailor Tech's Ecube is an electronic variant of a 3x3x3 cube made of RGB LEDs and switches instead of colored stickers and physically twisted in multiple layers. There are two switches in each row and each column. Press to indicate the direction of rotation and make the LED display change color to simulate a standard Rubik's cube rotation. The product was showcased at the Taiwan Government Academy Design Exhibition on October 30, 2008. Another electronic variant of the 3x3x3 Cube is Rubik's TouchCube. As you slide your finger across its face, its colored light pattern will rotate in the same way as on the mechanical cube. TouchCube is a fairly new product, launched at the American International Toy Fair in New York on February 15, 2009.

The Cube is the inspiration behind an entirely new category of puzzles, often referred to as zigzag puzzles. These other sets include the aforementioned cubes of different sizes and various other geometric shapes. Some of these forms include tetrahedron (Pyraminx), the octahedron (Skewb Diamond), the dodecahedron (Megaminx), and the icosahedron (Dogic). There are also deformation puzzles like Rubik's Cube Snake and Cube

One. With simpler deformations, the game style will change dramatically, and if you want to solve any changing cubes, your game style must also be the same.

Making origami

Origami originated in China and became popular in Japan. This is the art of origami. In Japanese, "ori" means fold, and "gami" means paper. What are the benefits of origami? The type of paper folding we are talking about here is different from simply folding a piece of paper into a pocket for easy carrying. The basic idea behind origami is the art of folding paper into various animals or objects, such as birds, butterflies, flowers, cups, buildings, robots, dogs, cats, and even Pokémon. Origami is more than just folding paper. It is a transformative paper. This is paper magic. Origami is even considered a form of art.

Origami can range from super complex models with realistic models to simple models that are easier to fold but easy to identify. No matter how complex, these models require carefully planned folding, just like the brush strokes in Rembrandt paintings. If you are like me, sometimes a random and awkward fold is enough to create something recognizable.

Origami is a hobby for all ages. All origami models vary in complexity, some being very simple and taking only three to five minutes, while some can be extremely complex and challenging, taking upwards of five hours. What is important when making origami is patience, as it can get very frustrating and unnerving, but with time and practice, you will master it in no time! No matter how old you are or your professional level, it will be fun. In the end, it is always magical. So, are you ready to fold your origami?

Although origami can be folded with various papers, the most common is folded with thin square paper because it can contain and support complex folds. If you want your model to look the best, you can buy pre-cut thin colored origami paper or make a square with ordinary 8.5x11 or A4 rectangular paper. The last option is to print colored origami and cut out squares.

Now all you have to do is find an origami model and fold it up! Here is some origami for you to choose from.

6.3 How to improve your memory and learning abilities

Our memory is an integral part of our identity, but our memory will deteriorate as we age. For many older people, the decline has become so severe that they can no longer live independently. This is one of the biggest fears adults have as they age.

The good news is that scientists have been learning more about the amazing ability of our brains to change and develop new neural connections every day, even into old age. This concept is called neuroplasticity. Through the study of neuroplasticity, scientists have discovered that our memory capacity is not fixed but flexible and malleable, much like plastic.

To take full advantage of neuroplasticity, you need to exercise your brain and take care of your body. In this chapter, we will cover twenty-four common tips which can help you boost your memory and learning capabilities.

1. Learn new things

Memory is like muscle power. The more you use it, the more powerful it will become. But you can not lift the same weight every day and expect to be stronger. You need to keep your brain under constant challenge. Learning a new skill is a great way to improve brain memory.

There are many activities to choose from, but most importantly, you need to find something that forces you to step out of your comfort zone and grab your full attention. Here are some examples:

- Learn a new musical instrument
- Make pottery
- Play intellectual games, such as Sudoku or chess
- Learn a new dance, such as Tango
- Learn a new language

2. Repetition and retrieval

Every time you learn new information, you are more likely to record that information in your mind if you repeat it. Repetition strengthens the connections we make between neurons. Repeat what you hear aloud. Try to use it in sentences. Write it down and read it aloud.

But the work does not stop there. Studies have shown that simple repetition alone is an ineffective learning tool. Later you will have to sit down and actively try to retrieve the information without looking at where you wrote the information. Testing yourself to retrieve information is better than repeated learning. Recall from practice can create a longer-term and more meaningful learning experience.

3. Try Acronyms, Abbreviations, and Mnemonics

Mnemonics can take the form of acronyms, abbreviations, songs, or rhymes. Since the 1960s, mnemonics have proven themselves as an effective student strategy. You may have learned some mnemonics to remember long lists. For example, the color of the spectrum can be remembered with the name ROY G. BIV (red, orange, yellow, green, blue, indigo, violet).

·   ·   ·

4. "Group" or "Block" Information

Group or block refers to dividing newly learned information into blocks to produce fewer and larger blocks of information. For example, you may have noticed that if you divide a 10-digit number into three separate parts (for example, 555-637-8299) instead of a long number (5556378299), it is easier to remember the phone number.

5. Build a "Mind Palace."

People with strong memory capabilities often use Mind Palace technology. In this ancient technology, you can create a complex and visual place to store a set of memories. To build a mind palace of your own, follow the steps below:

- Choose your palace

First, you must choose a place with which you are very familiar. Then, the effectiveness of this technique depends on your ability to visualize and mentally move around that place easily. Finally, you should be able to "be there" at will with just your mind's eye.

For example, a good first choice might be your own home. Remember, the more vividly you imagine the details of that place, the more effectively you can remember it.

Also, try to define specific routes in your palace instead of simply visualizing static scenes. Therefore, instead of just imagining your home, imagine a specific visit to your home. This makes the technique even more powerful because you will retrieve items in a specific order, as we will see in the next step.

Here are some additional suggestions for the Palace of Memory and possible routes:

- A familiar street in your city. The possible route might lead to work or any other street sequence that you are familiar with.
- Current or previous school. You can imagine the way from the classroom to the library (or to the bar across the street, but you are also if That is the route you remember).
- Workplace. Imagine the way from your cubicle to your boss's coffee machine or office (it should not be hard to choose).
- Imagine walking in a neighborhood near you or on a track you use when jogging in a local park.

- List the features of your palace

Now you need to pay attention to the details of the place you choose. For example, if you choose to visit your home, the first distinguishing feature might be the front door.

Now continue walking in your memory palace. What is in the first room after entering the door?

Analyze the room methodically (define a standard procedure, for example, always look from left to right). What is the next characteristic that caught your attention? It can be the center table of the restaurant, or it can be a picture on the wall.

Continue to write down these characteristics in my mind. Each of them will be a "memory slot" that you will use to store a piece of information.

- Print the palace in your mind

For technology to work, the most important thing is to print 100% of the location or route in your mind. Make every effort to truly remember it. If you are a visual person, you may not encounter this problem. Otherwise, here are some helpful tips:

The body crosses the path, loudly repeating the unique features it sees.

Write the selected functions on a sheet of paper, look for them in your heart and repeat them aloud. Make sure always to view entities from the same angle.

Please note that visualization is just a skill. If you still can not do this, you may need to develop your visualization skills first.

When you think you are done, check it again. How you "overlearned" yourself in your memory palace is important.

Once you are sure that the route is imprinted in your mind, you are good to go. Now that you have your palace, you can use it repeatedly to remember whatever you want.

- Associate with your palace

Since you are the owner, master, or lord of your palace, you should make good use of it.

Like most memory enhancement systems, memory palace technology uses visual associations. The process is simple: you take a familiar picture, called a memory pin, and combine it with the item you want to remember. For us, each memory nail is a distinctive feature of our memory palace. The memory tracking technique is the same as the technique described in the article "Improve your memory by speaking the language of your thoughts," so if you have not read it yet, I highly recommend that you do so.

There is a "right way" to make visual associations: Make crazy, absurd, offensive, unusual, extraordinary, vivid, absurd visualizations; after all, these are things that are easy to remember, are they not? Make the scene so unique that it will never happen in real life. The only rule is: if it is boring, it is wrong.

Although we can use this technique to memorize a lot of information, let us start with a very simple thing: use our memory palace "home" to memorize a shopping list. For example, suppose the first item in the list is "Bacon":

Transmit your spirit to your memory palace. The first feature you see in your mind is the front door. Now, in an absurd way, the "Bacon" is visually combined with the scenery of the front door. How about the big strips of fried bacon running from under the door to your lap, just like those zombies in the B movie? Feel the touch of the "bacon hand" on your leg. Smell the damn nasty bacon. Is it great?

Now open the door and continue walking, following the route you defined earlier. Take a look at the salient features below and associate them with the second item you want to remember. For example, suppose the next item is "eggs" and the second feature is "image of mother-in-law." Well, at this point, you know what to do. The process is always the same, so think about the image in your mind until there is nothing to remember.

- Visit your palace

At this point, you have completed the memory of the objects. However, if you are not familiar with this technology, you may need to rehearse and repeat the journey at least once in your mind.

6. Use all your senses

Another strategy for memory connoisseurs is not relying solely on one sense to help memorize information. Instead, they associate the information with other senses, such as color, taste, and smell.

7. do not go to Google right away.

Modern technology has its place, but unfortunately, it makes us "mentally lazy." So before you pick up your phone and ask Siri or Google, be sure to try to retrieve information with your mind. This process helps strengthen the neural pathways in the brain.

8. Avoid using a GPS to guide you to places

Another common mistake is to rely on GPS every time you drive. Relying on responsive technology (like GPS) for navigation will shrink the part of our brain called the hippocampus, responsible for spatial memory, and transfers information from short-term memory to long-term memory. Poor hippocampal health is linked to dementia and memory impairment.

Unless you are completely lost, try using your brain to get to your destination instead of just following the GPS directions. Maybe you use GPS to get there, but use your brain to get home. Your brain will thank you for the added challenge.

9. Stay busy

A busy schedule can keep the brain's episodic memory. A study links busy schedules with better cognitive function. However, this research is limited by self-reporting.

10. Stay organized

People who are organized are easier to remember. The checklist is a good organizational tool. Writing your list manually (rather than electronically) also increases the likelihood of remembering what you wrote.

11. Regular sleep

Go to bed at the same time every night and get up at the same time every morning. Try not to break the routine on weekends. Doing so can greatly improve the quality of your sleep.

12. Avoid bright screens before going to bed

The blue light emitted by mobile phones, TVs, and computer screens can inhibit the production of melatonin, which is a hormone that controls the sleep-wake cycle (circadian rhythm). Improper sleep cycle regulation can affect your sleep quality.

13. Improve and make changes to your diet

The Mediterranean diet, DASH (diet method to prevent high blood pressure) and MIND diet (Mediterranean DASH intervention for neurodegenerative diseases), and other diets have some things in common. This includes its ability to improve memory and reduce the risk of Parkinson's and Alzheimer's. These diets focus on the following foods:

- Plant foods, especially green leafy vegetables and berries
- Whole grains
- Legumes
- Nuts
- Chicken or turkey
- Olive or coconut oil
- Herbs and spices
- Fatty fish (salmon and sardines)
- Red wine in moderate amounts

Fatty fish are a rich source of Omega 3 fatty acids. Omega 3 acids play an important role in the formation of nerves and brain cells. They are essential for learning and memory and have been shown to delay cognitive decline.

14. Remove certain foods from your diet

Proponents of the Mediterranean diet and the MIND diet recommend avoiding the following foods:

- Sugar
- Processed foods
- Butter
- Red meat
- Fried foods

- Salt
- Cheese

Sugar and fat are associated with impaired memory. A recent human study found that diets high in fat and sugar, common in Western diets, can damage the memory of the hippocampus. However, the research is based on questionnaires and surveys, which may not be as accurate.

15. Avoid Certain Medications

Although you must still take the medications prescribed by your doctor, remember to follow your doctor's instructions for changing your diet and lifestyle.

Some prescriptions, such as statins for high cholesterol, are linked to memory loss and "brain fog." Losing weight and eating healthier can also play a role in treating high cholesterol.

Other medications that can affect memory include:

- Antidepressants
- Anti-anxiety medications
- Medications for high blood pressure
- Sleep aids
- Metformin

Talk to your doctor about managing your medical condition, so you do not have to rely on prescriptions forever. If you are concerned about how the medicine will affect your memory, discuss your options with your doctor.

16. Exercise

Exercise has been shown to have cognitive benefits. It can improve the body's oxygen and nutrient supply and help create new cells in the brain essential for memory storage. In addition, exercise helps to increase the number of cells in the hippocampus. Exercise does not have to be vigorous. For example, walking is a good option.

17. Manage Stress

When you are under stress, your body will release stress hormones such as cortisol. Cortisol has been shown to greatly affect the brain's memory process, especially our ability to retrieve long-term memories from reliable sources. Animal studies even show that stress and depression can reduce credible sources in the brain.

18. Socialize

Human beings are social animals. Studies have shown that a strong support system is essential for our mood and brain health. A 2007 study found that people with very active social lives have slower memory decline. Talking to another person for 10 minutes has been shown to improve memory.

19. Hydrate regularly

Your brain is mainly composed of water. Water is technically used as a shock absorber for the brain and spinal cord. It helps our brain cells use nutrients. Therefore, a small amount of dehydration can have catastrophic effects. Mild dehydration has been shown to cause brain atrophy and memory impairment. The goal is to drink at least 8 to 10 cups a day, and if you are very active, you can drink more.

20. Drink coffee

Caffeine has been shown to improve memory and reduce the risk of Parkinson's and Alzheimer's. But this one has a warning. Too much caffeine intake or drinking it later in the day will have the opposite effect because it affects the sleep of sensitive people. Thus, you must make sure that you are drinking your coffee at an appropriate time, like in the morning or during the afternoon, but never in the evening.

21. Do not drink excessively

Moderate drinking does have a positive effect on memory, but please remember that moderate drinking means that women only drink one cup a day and men only drink two cups a day. Excessive drinking can negatively affect your ability to retain information and sleep.

22. Meditation

There is growing evidence that meditation is good for health. In addition, studies have shown that meditation helps improve various cognitive functions, such as concentration, concentration, memory, and learning ability. Meditation can rewire the brain and promote more connections between brain cells. There are several ways to meditate - find out which one is right for you.

23. Enjoying nature

Walking in nature is very important for our physical and emotional health. Enjoying nature is said to be considered a form of meditation as well. Compared to walking in the city, walking in the park can improve memory and concentration. It is also said that daily gardening can also reduce the risk of dementia.

. . .

24. Lose excess weight

People with more fat tissue consume less water than those with less fat tissue. Overweight human brain tissue also has fewer credible sources. The more overweight you are, the more likely your brain is to shrink and affect your memory.

SEVEN

INDEPENDENT THINKING

If you do not think for yourself, others may try to do it for you! Many people will be happy to tell you what to think. They want to guide you, control you and make decisions for you.

If you are not thinking for yourself, you may not be speaking for yourself, so others may step in to speak for you or explain to you in a way that you do not want.

If you do not think for yourself or share your unique ideas, you may not be contributing the value you can bring or feeling completely satisfied or engaged. In addition, when you do not have a voice, others will think you are irrelevant.

Being an independent thinker is important because, as Nancy Kline said, "The quality of everything we do depends on the quality of the thinking we do first." If you regurgitate or follow other people's ideas, it is not high-quality thinking. In our personal and work lives, ineffective thinking can lead to ineffective or even catastrophic decisions and actions; how many times have you read the news and wondered, "What are they thinking?"

However, some people often do not know they are thinking about something or do not have the courage, will, or energy to think for themselves.

Independent thinking is not always easy because it may involve risks, such as being unpopular, opposing the majority, or being seen as different or uncooperative. You will feel selfish.

The question "What do you think?" can make some people feel vulnerable, and in some cases, people may think that what they share will have terrible consequences. However, others always need to approve your ideas; no matter if there is clear evidence that they are smart, your ideas are inherently valuable.

In some cases, people avoid thinking or simply remain silent because they have developed learned helplessness, used to being told what to do or what to do so that they no longer know how to do it themselves.

This means creativity and more consideration in your choice. Very young children still do not know how to think for themselves because although they are creative, they have no life experience, and they have not learned to reason. For example, young children are teachers who want (and often get) independence, but not necessarily teachers of independent thinking. Children's decisions are not always wise! Therefore, one of the tasks of parents is to cultivate children's ability to think independently.

As we grow up, when we do not have parents or caregivers to guide our thinking, independent thinking becomes the core of all our relationships and life decisions.

Because in the complex world we live in, we need a lot of critical thinking skills—for example, curiosity, the ability to determine different options before acting, weigh the pros and cons, solve problems alone and with others, avoid being deceived, and develop unique Ideas and different perspectives bring our creativity and diversity into group thinking, confidently say yes or no, and choose and guide based on our feelings and values.

If you do not develop the ability to think independently, you may become a victim of other people's assumptions about you: you cannot think or cannot learn how to think. For example, I often hear the frustrating voice "People here can not think!" or "I have to tell him what to do because he just can not think of anything about himself!" Therefore, if you do not think independently, you may become The puppets in the theater of other people's lives or the victims in their own lives.

If you are an independent thinker, you are a creative, rigorous, and courageous person, able to think smartly, have originality, be willing to take risks, focus on what is important to you, and understand others and their needs and perspectives.

7.1 How to become an independent thinker

Before we were born, the prejudices and beliefs of our parents had been downloaded to us. We are indoctrinated by influential people in our lives, such as our family, friends, teachers, trainers, and religious leaders. As a result, we tend to fall into the trap of obeying others instead of questioning and thinking for ourselves.

Traveling the world immediately takes us out of our comfort zone and allows us to appreciate our country more. It broadens our horizons and allows us to see new lifestyles, traditions, new people, environments, and activities that may never have been found in our homeland. Think of the most beautiful places in the world, such as the Ice Hotel in Sweden, the Giant Buddha of Leshan in China, Mont Saint-Michel in France, or the Blue Hole of Dean in the Bahamas.

Exploration involves constantly doing new things to discover new talents and abilities. As humans, we tend to look for more of the same operations on autopilots. Watch the same kinds of movies, attend certain concerts, read specific books, and talk to like-minded people. Doing the same activities will limit your chances in life.

When you learn new topics and engage in new activities, you will learn more about yourself, others, and the world, thereby gaining new insights and expanding your current level of thinking.

There are a million opportunities in the world, but when we limit ourselves, we miss what may be one of the best moments in our lives.

As Warren Buffet explained: "Fear when others are greedy and greedy when others are afraid." Although Buffett's famous saying applies to investing, it is also closely related to life. Take action in the way that suits you, instead of just going with the flow.

Entrepreneurs know this well. Because they will not blindly follow the crowd to work for paychecks, they have blazed their own trail. One of the main reasons why entrepreneurs put forward their own business is the ability to make their own decisions.

Be curious and strive to learn more. Ask any parent, and they will tell you how good their child is in asking about anything. People commonly enjoy talking about themselves and their experiences. When you show genuine interest and listen to their stories, you will learn a lot of information that can challenge your values, beliefs, and outlook on life. It is said that curiosity makes life interesting. Every day provides another reason to smile, another lesson to learn, another reason to be grateful, and another discovery.

I think most people do not like to be challenged on their values and beliefs. Provides benefits because when we participate in these conversations, we discover more about ourselves and others. If you stick with people who simply say you want to listen, you eliminate the growth that you have experienced.

7.2 Why should you be an independent thinker?

Independent thinkers are not common in today's culture, but based on their qualities, there are good reasons to be independent thinkers. Even if independent thinking is not natural for you, thinking outside the box has some benefits, in addition to the generally accepted ones. If you know someone who thinks independently, you probably know how smart they are and how they question everything. Here are some good reasons to become an independent thinker who can make your gears work!

. . .

One of the best reasons to become independent thinkers is that many are constantly seeking truth, not necessarily the usual truth. Our world and our culture are constantly changing, and every day we discover previously unknown things. Find the truth for yourself by reading, researching the evidence, and understanding the difference between biased information and reliable information. Achieving one's sense of accomplishment is much more satisfying than simply accepting the ideas of the masses.

People who believe in their mental abilities are always thinking, exploring, and imagining in their minds. Independent thinkers are visionaries. They lead the way to new systems, ignore fashion trends and norms, and explore new ways of doing things by learning how to make them better and more efficient. These visionaries are also innovative. Think of creative people like Steve Jobs, Bill Gates, Dave Packard, Bill Hewlett, and Mark Zuckerberg. All these creative people are/are ambitious innovators who think independently!

Maintaining independence and self-confidence in your intelligence means that you will exude self-confidence. You understand their abilities and are confident in their strengths. Confidence is always an ideal attribute. It makes a person have a high degree of employability, trustworthy and efficient ability. Also, remember to be humble because no one likes people who are overconfident and arrogant. On the contrary, be humble to ensure your advantages, and do not let your wisdom and abilities take over!

Have you ever met someone who creates new styles or regards one's opinions as absolute truth? These people are easily swayed by information full of misinformation. It is best to be an interrogator and think for yourself before drawing a clear conclusion about what is true or may be true. It can be said that when you think independently and do not automatically accept everything you hear, your thoughts are like a filter.

It is safe to say that we all like to be seen as unique individuals with different talents and attributes, which makes us different! In other words, it is easy to fall into pop culture trends and stick to "hot." Instead, try thinking about changing fashion trends, popular hobbies and activities, and new and increasingly popular lifestyles, such as medicine, food, or sports trends. Although these new trends can be interesting to explore, independent thinkers do not like to follow normal or "inside" things. They are unique in their approach to life and the way they cope with it. So choose what is good and interesting for you, regardless of what other people are doing.

Independent thinkers are people who analyze everything and have a strategic meaning to move forward! Being an independent thinker means you can assess the situation faster with clear thinking before moving on, which means fewer delays and higher productivity. Who does not want that?

Finally, one of the best qualities of independent thinkers is their constant search for knowledge. This is the goal that we should all strive for; even after graduating from college, knowledge is structured. Take time to learn new things, read books and articles, and get as much information as possible.

You may think that being an independent thinker is the opposite of being a critical thinker, but that is not true. Being an independent thinker means that you value your thoughts and opinions and do not let other people steer you and make up your thoughts themselves. On the other hand, critical thinking revolves more around synthesis and information gathering to reach a conclusion. You initially start with a critical thinking process, but it is often recommended that you continue with a more independent point of you so that you can properly and confidently get your thoughts across, without letting them get lost in the aether of other conversations and thoughts.

7.2 Knowledge management

Knowledge management (or KM) systems are all the rage recently. Using various tools to collect information from bookmarks and blog posts and connect it to a "personal wiki" can help you see your ideas from a different perspective. Linking your notes and ideas can bring huge benefits, not only for lifelong learners but also for anyone who wants to perform the best creative work.

But before you can take full advantage of personal knowledge management applications and services, you need to have a little understanding of how they work.

What do we understand by the term knowledge management? Knowledge Management (KM) is an information-gathering process. People use this information in their daily activities to collect, classify, store, search, retrieve and share knowledge and work in a way compatible with these processes Activities. In essence, knowledge management is a combination of two other concepts:

information management (IM) and knowledge management (KM).

You may already be familiar with Information Management (IM). Basically, this is how you get and retain information to help you get your job done. For example, you may need the information to be emailed to you to complete a job task. If you email your task manager, they have the email URL when you need it; that is information management.

Another concept you need to understand is knowledge management. This generally refers to the creation or sharing of knowledge and information within the organization. If you create standard operating procedures so that others can complete organizational tasks, this is a form of knowledge management. It is about ensuring the free flow of information, the required knowledge is not isolated, and others can access it when needed.

Knowledge management combines t but emphasizes sharing and creation. It is a structure of information and ideas that enables the two to connect in different fields. This creates interesting connections, generates new ideas, and greatly facilitates the creative process, whether expressed through writing, music, or any other medium.

. . .

What kind of knowledge does KM use to manage anyway? Let us start with the dictionary definition of knowledge: facts, information, and skills acquired through experience or education.

This is very broad and can mean many different things. For example, you may have vague memories of statistics that you read in a book, but you need to do a Google search to remember the true meaning. Or you can have a favorite quote, it speaks to you, and you built your values around it.

There are several different levels of knowledge:

Level 1: Having something (information) - Much of our digital information falls into this category. You can find what you are looking for when you need it, but you need to think about it before finding it. If you have a video course purchased but not completed, it falls into this category.

Level 2: Understand something (revelation): it is to be able to remember something without looking for it. You have internalized information and started making connections at this level, but this does not necessarily change the way you behave.

Level 3: Do Something (Application) - This is where you start to see the results of the information you collect. Not only do you own or understand it, but you are also changing your daily behavior. This is the first level, and you can see the real and visible result of the information you collect.

FOMO (fear of missing out) is obtaining information that is not currently available. But once you get it, you may feel FOMO about other things, such as Twitter, Facebook, email, Slack, YouTube, etc. By quickly jumping from one entry to the next, you inspire their desire to understand what is happening, but you cannot contribute to the conversation. You must do something about the information and ideas you have collected. Like plants, you need to develop and nurture these ideas to understand what they can become. One way to incubate these ideas is to connect them with other people and see what happens.

A good knowledge management system reveals the connections between information. When you give your brain time and space to think, it is already very good at this. The problem is that you are easily overwhelmed by anything urgent, and remembering things from a long time ago is terrible.

KM helps overcome these genetic weaknesses by acting as an external brain. It allows you to see existing connections and establish new ones, which is valuable when you allow yourself to incubate these ideas for a long time.

Although the term KM has become very popular recently, it is nothing new. Knowledge management systems have existed for many years. Here are some examples:

- A Commonplace Book - a collection of notes, quotes, and anecdotes you want to remember.
- Mind Map
- Sketch

Some of the most prolific creators in human history have been using versions of personal knowledge management systems for hundreds of years. Technology just allows us to connect things in a powerful way.

Whether you are a writer, musician, writer, or engineer, you are creative. Creativity happens to be a system, much like everything else in life. There is an entrance, a process, and an exit. So if you do not see a lot of creative output, it does not mean you are missing something in your DNA. Instead, it means you need to change your input or process.

KM without creativity is believed to be a false fabrication. You might have had a similar situation where you were trying to play an instrument or hum a melody without reading notes or lyrics. Still, you realized that it has some kind of connection to another song and asked yourself, "what is wrong with me?" or "Why can I not create anything original?"

It is important to note that nothing is completely original. When someone creates something, they just connect the dots in new ways. In short, this is why you should use KM: it can help you connect ideas and facilitate your best creative work.

KM does not have only a single application. Rather, it is a series of interrelated applications to promote the spread of ideas across multiple fields. The goal is not to have isolated information but to share and link to it easily. Listed below will be the components that make up a successful KM system:

Take notes: You need a place to collect text-based notes about things you want to remember. Some examples include notes from work meetings, quotes you like, or article ideas you want to recall later.

Quick capture: you need a tool that allows you to capture the idea the moment you have it so as not to lose it. If you can not capture an idea when it comes up, you will most likely forget it. Therefore, your quick-fit tool must have minimal friction.

Visual Thinking - This is just one way of looking at the relationship between ideas. A common example is a mind map of a topic in MindNode or a graphical view in applications like Roam or Obsidian. Visual thinking tools allow you to eliminate the memory methods we usually use in notes and make connections that we might not see.

Project Management - Whether you are a "knowledge worker" or an enterprise desktop contributor, you need a way to turn ideas into tasks. If you have many tasks and projects to manage, you may need a dedicated task management application. Just make sure you can easily put things in, take things out, and be connected to other parts of the PKM.

Archiving - This is an easy place to store items after they have been processed. Do not delete things! Move them to your archive. You may not need to go back to the file often, but it is important to find something later if you do.

Exit information or output - Remember, your knowledge management system should be easy for you to create. If there is no way out, then something is broken. After connecting your points, you need a way to express them. This may be a bunch of different formats, but the most popular starting point may be writing (even for videos).

You can choose to add many other parts to your PKM, but do not overcomplicate things. The simplest solution is usually the best solution.

Also, do not try to accomplish all of this with one application. The best apps are those that do only a few things but do a good job. You can quickly take notes in Drafts, manage projects in Things, do mind maps in MindNode, and complete all writing (output) in Ulysses. This is a very effective method of personal knowledge management.

Just make sure you have a way to connect things between these different applications so that your ideas can flow between them easily.

No matter which methods you decide to use, you need to keep the following points in mind when creating a KM system:

Cultivate your collection

An easy mistake to make at the beginning is to try to connect everything. But not every idea or new information you find is worth recording on your PKM. To get the most out of your network of ideas, you need to manage them by keeping the information relevant and discarding the useless stuff. It may take some time to discover the difference, but it is worth finding out.

Complement your workflow

do not change everything just because you want to try a brilliant new application. If You have been using Evernote as a collection point for years and have hundreds of informational notebooks, then moving everything to another app is a significant time investment. Seek to simplify your information workflow so that the applications you already use can better communicate with each other.

Consider your source of information

As we mentioned earlier, there is too much information to keep up with everything. Therefore, find out which sources deserve special attention. By limiting the number of blogs you follow or the number of websites you read regularly, you can get more information from the new information you receive. As the quantity decreases, the quality will naturally increase.

KM is still, to this day, a topic that is constantly in development, especially with new technologies and methods which can be implemented, such as new apps and note-taking methods, which either make accumulating information easier or make storing information a breeze. Regardless of how much easier the process becomes, you should never be too laid-back and relaxed, as information is always floating around you in one way or another.

7.3 Executive visioning: how to spot problems to solve

Executive visioning is a very sought-after quality - we are talking about a rare quality that elevates people above others. Getting to big places involves more than just studying hard, working long hours, and waiting for big opportunities, as cultivating leadership is not easy. The running pyramid becomes very narrow at the top, so only the smartest and best people can reach it. To become a CEO or managing director, you need to have a wealth of leadership skills, vision, and motivation, but you also need special creative sparks.

Many times, the ability to solve problems, the ability to face difficult challenges, and the ability to make the right decisions under pressure separate the wheat from the chaff. Of course, no one can see the future and imagine what is about to happen, whether in business or life. But, in many ways, top managers are responsible for doing this, which can be one of the most desirable roles.

Your job is to identify opportunities and risks, predict future trends, and formulate strategic directions for the organization. If they are successful, they and the people who work for them will be praised and rewarded. However, when business leaders choose the wrong course of action, things do not go according to plan, this will be seen as their responsibility, and their minds are ready.

When solving problems on the board, business leaders must consider goals and obstacles. What are your short-term and long-term goals for the organization, and what obstacles might hinder success? Senior managers need to have a vision and a clear mind to identify these challenges and then choose the course of action to bring the most beneficial results.

Generally speaking, the overall goal of business is to maximize the organization's profits, thereby maximizing the profits of shareholders. But to achieve this goal, it is necessary to achieve a series of small goals. For example, to increase profits, the company may need to improve service quality, increase productivity, increase customer loyalty, participate in employee retention, and identify new efficiencies to reduce costs.

There are many different ways to achieve the same result, and it is the job of senior management to determine the best method in each case. They must foresee obstacles to success and think creatively to eliminate them. If this is not possible, they may need to develop completely new ways to solve the problem.

Sometimes, the role of top managers is to solve problems quickly and quickly reach the same conclusions as others, given all the relevant information, but in a short time. This can give your organization an advantage in the business because it can be more agile and act while rival operators are still considering the best way forward.

Although leadership styles can vary, top business leaders can quickly identify potential problems, conduct the necessary research and analysis, and make decisions. Of course, they must have excellent business intuition and the courage to affirm beliefs. But they also need to be pragmatic enough to realize that they will not always have answers and will need to seek help in the process.

Senior managers must use the expertise of everyone working for their organization, sometimes even outsiders. People with expertise may be better able to judge the pros and cons of a particular decision, so it makes sense to consult them. The job of the managing director or CEO is to decide the final approach and be responsible for their decisions. Still, they can understand the specific challenges before reaching this stage.

Similarly, senior managers can use technology solutions to improve the decision-making process. In the digital age, organizations collect and store more and more data, which can be analyzed to obtain information and business intelligence. It is the responsibility of decision-makers to interpret this data and plan appropriate actions accordingly.

Decisions made by senior business leaders can affect all stakeholders in the organization, including board members, employees, shareholders, and customers. Therefore, your responsibilities are heavy.

They need to use available resources (including the data and experience of others) to make decisions, but sometimes their main assets will be their skills, judgment, and intuition. Over time, they will be evaluated based on the results of their actions or inactions.

Future career prospects, and even the sustainable viability of enterprises and organizations, may depend on the decision of the company's boss. Therefore, there is no doubt that senior management positions are under pressure. However, professionals need a little more to succeed in such a role.

AFTERWORD

With this chapter, it is time to conclude the contents of this book and hopefully help you set sail on an amazing and thrilling journey of self-development.

Starting from the very beginning, where we learned about the history and basics of critical thinking, what it is and what goal it has in our lives, through the various other skills that you can learn along with it to complement it, such as self-discipline, where we talked about managing our emotions and urges, increasing our productivity and how to deal with negative emotions, or problem-solving, where we covered various ways of how to go about solving problems of varying scales effectively. We also tackled how to make decisions efficiently and how important a skill it is, especially in professional environments. Another topic we talked about was reasoning, how to go about it, how hobbies help with reasoning and how our memory plays a large part in it, and how keeping it functioning is of great importance. Finally, we worked on independent thinking, the importance of having your thoughts, and the importance of being an independent thinker, but also two very important topics that coincide with it, more specific knowledge management to help us retain the information we acquire daily and how to spot problems that need solving effectively.

It is of utmost importance that you do not see this book as your sole source of information and guidance that you will adhere to at all times. With each passing day, things change, and new information can be found everywhere. We mentioned how important it is to be curious, so make sure to keep your mind entertained by constantly searching for new knowledge and ways to better yourself.

With all of this in mind, we would like to express our sincerest gratitude for choosing this book in particular as your source of information and as your initial guide towards your first steps to becoming a more amazing person than you already are. We would be very glad if you took some of your free time to give this book a positive rating. By doing so, you massively contribute to the chance that another curious individual like yourself finds it and begins a journey of self-development much like you.

Made in the USA
Coppell, TX
19 September 2021